HOW TO RUN YOUR OWN HOME BUSINESS

Coralee Smith Kern
Tammara Hoffman Wolfgram

VGM Career Horizons
a division of *NTC Publishing Group*
Lincolnwood, Illinois USA

Library of Congress Cataloging-in-Publication Data

Kern, Coralee Smith.
  How to run your own home business / Coralee Smith Kern, Tammara
Hoffman Wolfgram.

     p.   cm.
  Includes bibliographical references.
  ISBN 0-8442-6666-3 : $7.95
  1. New business enterprises. 2. Home-based businesses. 3. Self
-employed. I. Wolfgram, Tammara Hoffman. II. Title.
HD62.5.K465   1989
685' .041—dc20   89-39354
                                          CIP

1992 Printing

Published by VGM Career Horizons, a division of NTC Publishing Group.
© 1990 by NTC Publishing Group, 4255 West Touhy Avenue,
Lincolnwood (Chicago), Illinois 60646-1975 U.S.A.

2 3 4 5 6 7 8 9 0 VP 9 8 7 6 5 4

About
the
Authors

Coralee Smith Kern is an at-home business woman, publisher of the *Mind Your Own Business at Home* newsletter, founder of the not-for-profit National Association for the Cottage Industry which was recently reorganized as the International Association for Home Business. In 1983 she was named the Illinois Small Business Woman of the year.

Since 1970 Ms. Kern has been owner-manager of a successful at-home business, Maid-to-Order, which has grown into a major maid and party service in the Chicago area. She publishes the *Mind Your Own Business at Home* newsletter for the home business person, offering advice and helpful information on subjects such as business organization methods, marketing, promotion, and family assistance. Her newsletters include expert counsel provided by accountants, attorneys, insurance brokers, financial consultants, and government agencies. Recognizing the need for a clearinghouse of information for home-based cottage industries, Ms. Kern recently formed the Center for the Study of the Cottage Industry.

For a number of years Ms. Kern has conducted seminars and workshops that provide firsthand business problem solving and allow both men and women to explore new home business opportunities. Her contributions in the work-at-home field include authoring the Small Business Administration's *Home Business Bibliography,* representing cottage industries at the Illinois Small Business Conference, and speaking on the issue to the World Future Society. She has appeared on more than seventy radio and television talk shows, testified at the U.S. Senate hearing on home business, and was one of seven people invited to participate in a think tank on home-based businesses in Stamford, Connecticut.

Tammara Hoffman Wolfgram has worked for the National Association for the Cottage Industry since the beginning of 1983 and for the Center for the Study of the Cottage Industry since its inception. During that time she helped organize several regional conferences and has written several home business workshops which have been presented to numerous organizations, colleges, and vocational schools across the country.

Following her work with a home business workshop presented in conjunction with the conference of the World Future Society in Washington, D.C., Ms. Wolfgram has had articles on subjects related to cottage industries published in *The Futurist, ProFiles,* and *Arthritis Today* magazines.

In her work with home businesses, Ms. Wolfgram has researched various aspects of cottage industries, particularly the psychological factors involved in working from home.

Having earned a bachelor's degree in psychology from the University of Wisconsin-Milwaukee, she is currently completing work on an advanced degree in education.

Acknowledgments

We would like to thank a number of people who, each in his or her own way, helped to make this book possible. Heartfelt thanks go to our families, especially to Marc, Jennifer, Gwendolyn, and Megan. Their patience and occasional sacrifices were important factors during the preparation of the manuscript. Patricia Hoffman deserves a very special thank-you. Her stylistic and editing suggestions were invaluable to this book. We are grateful for her tireless work.

Foreword

I started my business back in 1951 on my kitchen table, where it remained for two years until the business outgrew my small apartment. It was a no-cost way to keep overhead low so I could put my $2,000 of "venture capital"—my wedding gift money—into inventory. Plus, it allowed me to fulfill my other roles as a wife, mother, and homemaker.

Having my business at home gave me a lot of freedom and flexibility to set my own hours and to work when I needed to and wanted to. It worked for me and can work for you, also. Good luck in your home business venture!

Lillian Vernon Katz
Founder and Chief Executive Officer
Lillian Vernon Catalog Company

Preface

Working from home is an option which only recently has begun to be reexamined by our society. We tend to think of work stereotypically as earning a living by going to a forty-hour-per-week job in a central office, factory, or retail outlet, usually for a company with a large managerial structure. While particulars might vary, one aspect which seems unvarying is that work takes place at a location away from one's home.

This view is beginning to change as the nature of our economy and technology is changing. We are no longer dependent on face-to-face contact or conventional mail service to get things done. Telecommunications and the ability for computers to communicate and transmit documents via modems have dramatically changed our methods of business.

Then, too, we are witnessing a dramatic change in social roles in our society. Increasingly, women are joining the work force, and this includes mothers of young children. Fathers want to have a more active part in rearing their children. Working people of both sexes are demanding more from their jobs than mere monetary compensation. We now expect our work to be challenging, interesting, and fulfilling.

As we move from an industrial to an informational, service-oriented economy, fundamental changes are occurring in the types of jobs available. Moreover, entrepreneurship thrives during periods of great economic change such as we have been experiencing. Industrial corporations, the dinosaurs of our time, are being replaced by small, vibrant, quickly growing companies, many that are based on advanced technology.

Home-based businesses fit well with this new picture of work. They answer the needs of working parents, can meet the expectations we have of our jobs, and fit well with the changes in our economic structure. Home ventures are often an excellent route for the would-be entrepreneur.

The authors undertook the writing of this book with strong convictions about the efficacy of working at home and the growing importance of home businesses in our society. Both authors work from their homes, and they have been vocal advocates of the work-at-home movement.

They realize, of course, that a home-based occupation is not the right choice for everyone. The purpose of this book is to help you ascertain whether or not you would be well suited for a home-based occupation. It identifies the qualities needed by a home entrepreneur and examines what is necessary to set up and run a home business. Several types of home businesses are discussed, and the book attempts also to give the reader a sense of how home work fits into our society.

Contents

Cottage Industries in Today's Society

1

Working at home can hardly be called a new phenomenon. For centuries, in nearly every culture, people worked out of their homes. It has only been in the last century or so that society moved from an almost totally self-employed, at-home work force to a highly industrialized force, involving both specialization and centralization.

Within the past decade, however, a significant and increasing number of people have chosen to earn their livelihoods working at home. Let's examine this trend that appears to be gaining sufficient momentum to warrant being termed a social movement.

Historical Perspective

Historically, nearly all businesses were home businesses. Until the nineteenth century, the world's economy was primarily agricultural. With the majority of people living on farms or in small villages, it was necessary for the average family to be largely self-sufficient. Consequently, most people of the time grew or raised their own food and made their own clothing, shelter, and furniture. A small amount of manufacturing was done in the towns, largely by craftsmen who produced small amounts of goods such as hardware, guns, and some cloth. These manufactured goods from town were exchanged for food from the country districts. A certain amount of trade also existed for merchants of materials such as salt, spices, and other goods not readily available in the area.

Traditional cottage industries

Cottage industries, or the domestic system as it was also known, can be traced back as early as the 1200s. Since factories were virtually unknown until the 1800s, craftsmen of earlier centuries worked at home to produce goods for merchants or entrepreneurs. This system of producing goods was widely used in clothing, weaving, and other industries of the day.

The term *cottage industry* came into common usage during the Industrial Revolution. The original type of cottage industry consisted of a work arrangement between a worker and an entrepreneur. The worker agreed to make products, such as clothing, for the entrepreneur whose responsibility was then to sell those goods. Most commonly, the worker made the product in his home, thus giving rise to the term *cottage industry*. In this work arrangement, the worker was not the employee of the entrepreneur. Rather, he or she was paid for producing whatever goods had been agreed upon and could accept or refuse additional work. The entrepreneur owned the raw materials, paid for the work done, and took the risk of finding a market. Often such enterprises were spread out to include workers in several villages.

The Industrial Revolution initially spurred large growth in cottage industries. As machines were invented and harnessed, more workers than ever before were needed to make cloth and then to take that cloth and make it into clothing. Because the Industrial Revolution was in actuality an evolution, as one machine was invented and put to use, other aspects of production lagged behind in development. For example, even though a machine had been invented that could spin thread, it was a number of years before other machines were invented that could weave the thread into cloth or sew the cloth into clothing. Great numbers of home workers were thus engaged in clothing and other industries.

The factories of the 1800s were not large enough to house all of the workers, so factory owners sublet contracts for part of the work they needed done. Other manufacturers then set up makeshift factories with poor working conditions and very low wages, usually on a piecework basis. Although people began objecting to sweatshop conditions as early as 1830, it wasn't until the formation of unions that workers had any power or protection to better their working conditions and wages.

Decline of cottage industries

In the early 1900s, union pressure led states to begin to pass laws prohibiting workers from carrying on work outside the factories in industries where sweatshops were most common. Also contributing to the demise of cottage industries was the fact that heavy industry, such as steel and metalworking, which could not be carried on outside of the factory, became an important part of the economy.

The invention of heavy machinery, cheaper assembly-line production, and the development of unions and legislation designed to protect factory laborers—all contributed to the eventual centralization of most businesses. Centralized businesses made supervision of both workers and product quality easier for the business owner. Working on assembly lines with the aid of machines, workers made goods at a faster rate, and production was more cost efficient than having one person make each product from start to finish.

After restrictions against labor unions were lifted in the late 1860s, it was much easier for workers to organize in order to gain fair wages. With advantages for both the business owner and the workers, it seemed that centralized business was here to stay. And for the better part of a century, centralized industries and businesses have dominated the world of work.

As America became more of an urban, industrial society, earning money from home became an uncommon way to earn a living. Home business ventures were usually limited to people making supplemental money from hobbies such as woodworking or needlecrafts or earning some extra money in one's spare time by doing side jobs such as ironing, alterations, baby sitting, or house painting. Working from home was no longer looked on as a legitimate way of earning a living.

Following this trend, the federal Industrial Home Work Act of 1943 banned those areas of work that could most easily be done from home. While the intent of this act was to put a final damper on the exploitation of workers, primarily in the garment industry, this legislation had more far-reaching repercussions for home-based businesses. These repercussions will be discussed in a later chapter.

Rebirth of Home Business

Recently, we have been witness to a rebirth of the cottage industry. People all over the United States, and in other countries as well, have shown a resurging interest in working from home.

Home business ventures, at least in small number, have always existed. Traditionally these home businesses were the woman who took in sewing or ironing, the man who made wooden toys and furniture in his spare time, the baby-sitters, quiltmakers, and craftspeople who supplied all their neighbors with handmade gifts. There are many people who still do these activities from their homes.

Currently, home-based businesses encompass much, much more. Changes have occurred in our society and in the way people think of home businesses that have broadly expanded the types of businesses that are now run from home. The massive growth of computers in businesses, the emphasis in our economy on services and information, and the rising costs of office space, fuel, and corporate overhead have all contributed to the change.

However, the single most important aspect that has increased the range of home businesses is change in attitude. More and more people are recognizing the home not only as a legitimate place of business, but as the best place for their business needs.

The spectrum of home business people is ever broadening. Through alternate work site programs, many corporations now have employees who telecommute, working at least part of the time on computer terminals in their homes. Entrepreneurs are running tutoring services, maid services, and a wide range of secretarial services from their homes. Shopping and wardrobe consultants, caterers, writers, accountants, and real estate agents are all working from home. Even professionals such as business consultants, lawyers, engineers, and psychologists are working from home. In fact, the demographics of the people involved in working at home seem to be as divergent as the demographics found in the population at large.

Basic Definitions   To make discussion of home businesses easier, a number of terms need to be defined. These closely related terms are often confused: home-based business, home business, cottage industry, worksteader, entrepreneur, electronic cottage, and telecommuting.

Based on current usage, the terms *home-based business, home business,* and *cottage industry* may be regarded as interchangeable. Basically, all three terms refer to any business that is run from a residence. Most business analysts also include in this group businesses run from related buildings such as garages, studios, and barns. A person who works from home is often called a *worksteader* or *entrepreneur.*

Special designations are given to home work involving computers. An *electronic cottage* is a computerized home business, and *telecommuting* usually refers to working at home while being tied or connected to a main office via computer lines.

A home business is most often self-contained in one residence, but several at-home workers may be linked together in the same business. An example of the former is a woman who runs a completely self-contained real estate office in her home. The second type is exemplified by a group of people who manufacture toys using a piecework arrangement in different homes but who operate as a single business.

Also included in the definition of a cottage industry or home-based business is the person who is an employee of an outside company but who works at home either part or all of his or her working hours. Most current home work of this type involves computers and telecommuting. An excellent example of this type of work is a large catalog retailer in the Midwest that has computer terminals in employees' homes, enabling these home workers to take catalog orders for customers. These computers are tied to the mainframe computer, giving each employee access to all the information on the main computer. As computer use increases in our society, we will probably see this type of arrangement become more and more common.

Sizes and Kinds of Businesses   While the majority of home enterprises are classified as small businesses, they range considerably in size. Most home businesses employ only one or a few people, but it is not unheard of for certain types of home businesses to employ thirty or more workers.

The types of home businesses are virtually limitless. Although, at first glance, it might seem that very few businesses would be well suited to being run from residences, there are currently businesses of every variety being run from home. These ventures vary from animal grooming to psychiatry, real estate, carpentry, upholstery, dentistry, light manufacturing, child care, and law practice. In fact, while certain businesses may require special arrangements in order to be operated from the home, the kind of business you can operate from a dwelling is limited only by your creativity and imagination.

Cottage Industry Facts and Figures

Statistics on the prevalence of home business have become more accurate in the last few years. Probably the best estimate of the size of the home business sector comes to us from the United States Chamber of Commerce. The U.S. Chamber of Commerce estimates that as many as 23 million Americans have set up money-making enterprises at home, which represents a 50% increase in the last decade. A survey by AT&T shows that 13% of all households in the U.S. house a business. More than half of these businesses are full-time operations that provide the bulk of household income.

A Link Resources survey shows that of America's 116 million working people, 24 million work at home, which represents a 3 percent increase over 1987. Further, the Link study showed that 4.3 million earn all their income at home, representing a 20 percent increase in one year. According to Raymond Boggs, director of small business marketing strategy for CAP International, 28 million people work at home at least part of the time. This represents 35 percent of the total work force.

In the last five to ten years, interest in home business has spawned quite a bit of study and research. From this research, three distinct groups of home workers have emerged. The largest segment, 14 million, work outside the home each day but bring some portion of their work home. The second segment of home workers includes those people for whom their home business represents the second income of a household. There are about 11 million of these free-time entrepreneurs. The third group of home workers, numbering about 3 million, consists of home businesses that are the sole or major source of income for the household.

The size and subsequent impact of the work-at-home

movement have been largely underestimated. There are several reasons for the disparity in estimates related to the number of home businesses. First, government and other agencies have usually lumped cottage industries together with other small businesses. As a result, their importance in the economy was mistakenly viewed as insignificant. Only in the last few years have cottage industries received serious attention from government and the media.

Second, for a number of reasons, home business people often prefer to use an address other than their home address for their business. Frequently they use a post office box or other mailing address.

A third reason is that many home businesses are part-time efforts entered into by people working outside the home at a primary job, so the income from the home business is reported as supplemental income. In another variation, a great many people maintain a home office and an outside office for the same business and work at home only a portion of their week.

Finally, there are a variety of home businesses whose owners have never considered themselves to be home businesses because the business is carried on outside the home, such as plumbing, painting, and grading services. It is easy to overlook this segment of home business. Yet, if you further investigate the majority of these businesses, you'll find that they do indeed use their homes as the base of their business operations.

Various estimates of the number of people in the at-home movement at present range from thirteen million to twenty-eight million. Again, there are no official demographic figures on home business workers, since this area of business has only recently begun to obtain national recognition.

As this book is being written, government-funded research is being undertaken to gather further information about the following items.

- Who is working from home, including age, sex, and ethnic groups.

- What type of businesses they are in.

- Where, in terms of geographic location, home businesses are most prevalent.

- Amount of money generated by such businesses.

Clearly, this information will be extremely useful to many individuals, educational institutions, government agencies, and private businesses.

Home Businesses and You

Home-based businesses can be exciting and challenging alternatives to traditional types of employment. No doubt you are reading this book because you find the concept of working from home interesting and want to know more about home businesses. Perhaps you are considering or actually planning a home business of your own.

Home businesses are tremendously diverse. They currently exist in nearly every field, from accounting to yoga instruction. Moreover, since so many different types of businesses can be run from home, there is a great deal of flexibility regarding the skills and training needed. Whatever your interests and abilities are, you can tailor a home business career to fit them.

The remainder of this book is devoted to exploring the different aspects of working from home. We have included qualities needed to run a home business, fundamentals of home business, information about different types of cottage industries, and worksheets to help you select and plan your business, as well as current trends in home business. If you are considering the possibility of working from home, this book can help you to decide whether a home business is right for you. If you have already decided to start a home business, this book can help you give your business a great start.

Preparing to Run a Home-based Business

Anyone preparing to run a home-based business needs to learn a great deal to assure the best possible chance for success. If you are contemplating beginning a cottage industry or if you already have one and want to strengthen it, knowledge can mean the difference between success and failure or between a marginal and highly profitable venture. You need to study yourself, your product or service, and sources of information and help.

Are You Well Suited to Working at Home?

Not everyone is equally suited to working at home. What attributes appear to be needed? What qualities and skills do you possess? How can working at home meet special needs or goals of some individuals?

Basically, all successful entrepreneurs share certain attributes. Some of these may be more important than others, depending on the individuals and the businesses involved. A number of these qualities and skills tend to overlap one another. Remember also that all of these factors may not be present from the beginning of the venture. Many can be developed or learned. Nevertheless, all of these factors are important to some degree in starting and maintaining a successful home business endeavor.

Necessary personal attributes

Independence. Perhaps most important in meeting the demands of working at home is the ability to work well independently. In a conventional job, an employee nearly always has a boss and co-workers who provide not only the impetus to get a job done but also encouragement, criticism, praise, and daily support of a worker's efforts. Much of this type of support is lacking at home, so it is crucial that a home business worker is a self-starter and able to provide her or his own feedback.

Many home businesses are one-person ventures. It is very important that the worker like functioning predominantly alone. Of course, there are many people who run home businesses while family members are present or who see customers or other business contacts on an occasional or frequent basis. But being able to work well alone is still an important consideration for success. People who feel that there are too many distractions in an office, those who come in early or stay late, or who take work home because they can accomplish more when nobody is around probably would do quite well working in a home atmosphere.

Entrepreneurial spirit. One of the most essential qualities for a person running a home business is the entrepreneurial spirit. Entrepreneurs are people who are willing to take calculated risks. If you are the type of person who has to have guarantees up front, then starting a home business is probably not for you. In any business, there is a certain risk of failure. No business is immune to this. To be sure, there are a number of things you can do to lower the risk, such as researching your business thoroughly before starting, but the element of risk still exists.

Creativity. Home business workers need to be creative or imaginative. Even more than in a traditional business, creative problem solving, imaginative marketing strategies, and original ideas are important to give your business the competitive edge it will need in order to succeed.

Even the most elemental aspect of selecting your type of business can be greatly enhanced if you approach the question creatively. By thinking of novel approaches or unusual products, it is quite possible to find an untapped market. A woman in Wisconsin, for example, came up with an idea for health-food gourmet dog biscuits. This original thinker now runs a highly successful business.

Hard work. Another important quality, especially in early stages when the business is just getting established, is the ability to work hard. While home businesses may vary in their goals, those entrepreneurs intending to make a full-time living from their home business should realize that working from home will require more effort and probably more time than working at a conventional job.

Since most home businesses are run entirely by one or two people, you are responsible for everything from conceiving of the product or service to marketing and promotions, keeping the books, and taking out the garbage. While it is very true that home businesses generally can be shaped to fit the needs and goals of the individual, in no way should home business be viewed as an easier way to "make a buck" than a conventional job.

Business knowledge. The majority of small business failures are directly attributable to lack of business knowledge and experience. Unfortunately all too many people start businesses blindly without doing any research or having any real knowledge of what it actually takes to run a home business. Lacking information and experience about bookkeeping, taxes, zoning laws, marketing, and other areas vital to a successful business, they are dooming their businesses to failure almost before they begin.

Experience in business is invaluable to anyone desirous of starting a home business. If you don't have this type of experience, then it is imperative that you get at least an informal education in running a business. What you need to know is discussed in more detail in subsequent chapters. The important thing is to be willing to learn everything you can about running your business. If you don't know about a particular aspect of running a business, take the time to research it until you do.

Organizational skills. The ability to plan and organize is extremely important for the worksteader, especially since he or she is responsible for a wide range of business activities. While it isn't necessary to be so well organized that every piece of paper is always in place, successful home entrepreneurs have the ability to plan their time and organize their activities. Being able to adhere to a schedule and develop a system of organization for your papers and other working materials will enable you to make effective use of your time.

Perseverence. Another necessary quality for the home business person to possess is perseverance or persistence. Many people you will encounter will not necessarily take a home business seriously nor empathize with your needs. Consequently, it may take more effort to get financial backing or to have your business be accepted by the community at large. You need to be persistent in your attempts to get your business off the ground. You cannot allow minor setbacks or negative feedback to sway you from your goals.

Assertiveness. The quality of assertiveness or bold initiative will help assure that your business grows. A home business person can't sit back passively and wait for the business to start taking off. As a worksteader, you must take the initiative and not be timid about selling yourself or your product to prospective clients. After all, if you look at the most successful companies in your area, most of them are quite boastful of their products and services. If you don't have confidence in the quality of what you do, you can scarcely expect customers to feel any differently.

Decision-making skills. One important area of running your own business is the ability to make quick, accurate decisions and then act on those decisions. In order to run a business smoothly, a myriad of decisions must be made. You need to be able to gather pertinent information, analyze your choices, and make a decision, often in very little time. If you vacillate, you run the risk of losing valuable opportunities. Good decision-making skills, on the other hand, can help your business grow and flourish.

Leadership. While having leadership qualities can be valuable for any home worker, it is particularly important for those entrepreneurs who have people working for them. It is important to be a forceful leader who inspires confidence and loyalty in subordinates.

Responsibility. There are few undertakings which have more demands than running your own business. As a home business person you will need to accept responsibility for nearly every aspect of your business. This means being responsible for things that may go wrong, as well as taking care of the many duties your business demands.

People person. Successful home business people are able to deal with people honestly, positively, and show a genuine interest in those around them. When you are truly concerned about those around you, it shows both in the way you treat people and in the quality of work you do for others. Your customers will notice and appreciate the time and care you take to make sure their needs are met.

Achievement-oriented person. The majority of successful entrepreneurs thrive on setting difficult goals and then striving to achieve them. If you want to succeed in a home business, you must be the type of person who sets your sights high, then works to achieve and even surpass your goals. If you are this kind of person, there is virtually no limit to what you can achieve.

Management skills. In addition to knowledge of business, home business people must possess good management skills. To run a business successfully, you need to manage resources such as time, money, and people to their best advantage. This also includes keeping careful business records. The more efficiently run a business is, the greater its chances for success.

Communication skills. If you want to successfully sell your product or service, you need to communicate effectively. The ability to speak and write persuasively is crucial if you want to show customers the advantages of your product or service. Being able to say things clearly and succinctly is also helpful in dealing with people in all aspects of your business.

Necessary Personality Traits

For each of the following statements, give yourself 2 points if the statement is very true, 1 point if it is somewhat true, and 0 points if it is not true about you at present.

_____ 1. **Independence**
I feel my independence is very important, and I am motivated to work without the urging of others.

_____ 2. **Entrepreneurial Spirit**
I am willing to take calculated risks with my property when I have a chance to gain by doing so.

_____ 3. **Creativity**
I enjoy experimenting with new ideas, to invent or innovate in order to improve on the status quo.

_____ 4. **Hard Work**
I am willing to work hard for long hours to get something I really want.

_____ 5. **Business Knowledge**
I have ample experience and knowledge in the type of work I plan to do.

_____ 6. **Organizational Skills**
I am highly capable of planning and organizing in a logical order after examining the business from all angles.

_____ 7. **Perseverance**
I am willing to sacrifice, overcome obstacles, and work consistently to achieve a goal.

_____ 8. **Assertiveness**
I seek out new challenges, confident that I can meet and overcome obstacles.

_____ 9. **Decision-making Skills**
After considering the information available to me, I am able to make quick and accurate decisions.

_____ 10. **Leadership**
I am a forceful leader who inspires confidence and loyalty in those I lead.

_____ 11. **Responsibility**
I seek out and welcome responsibility.

_____ 12. **People Person**
I deal with people honestly and positively, and I am genuinely interested in others.

_____ 13. **Achievement-oriented Person**
I enjoy setting difficult goals, attaining them, and then moving on to more difficult challenges.

_____ 14. **Management Skills**
I manage resources such as money, people, and time to their best advantage, keeping careful and accurate records.

_____ 15. **Communication Skills**
I can write and speak clearly and persuasively.

Total Points

The possible range of points is from 0-30. The higher your score, the better your personality is suited to running a home business.

You make the difference

Certain types of businesses require different personal attributes than others. Some businesses, for example, may require a great deal of assertiveness, while others may allow less assertiveness but demand a great deal of hard work. Many businesses depend on a high degree of creativity; others demand extremely good organization and attention to details.

While these personal qualities and skills may seem like a lot to expect of any one individual, remember that many of these attributes can be developed or strengthened by a person who feels a lack in some area. Keep in mind also that it is not necessary to be the most assertive, persistent person you know. Possessing these qualities to some degree is all that is necessary.

You may feel that you need to develop or strengthen some personality traits or personal skills in order to be more successful in your home business. If so, take action. Develop some goals and work on them until you have accomplished your goals. The following worksheet can be used both to develop untapped personality traits and to learn skills necessary to run your business.

Goals for Personal Growth

Characteristic I Would Like to Change.	How Will I Change or Work around the Characteristic?	When Would I Like These Changes to Occur?
I don't know anything about keeping business records	Hire an accountant. Read books on it. Take a course.	Immediately. By the end of May. In six months.

Decision-making Skills

One area in which many would-be entrepreneurs can improve their skills is in the decision-making process. Unfortunately, too many people have difficulty in making decisions. In fact, many of us become paralyzed in our decision making lest we make the wrong decision.

An important step in the decision-making process is to gather information about the topic that will enable you to make a sound, knowledgeable decision. Sources of information will vary widely, depending on the decision to be made. Reference books, books on running a business, financial newspapers, trade journals, colleagues, and your own research all can be helpful sources of facts.

Once you have studied the available information, develop several alternative solutions. Perhaps the most common mistake people make when trying to arrive at a decision is in assuming that there are only two alternatives for any problem. For example, "Either I get this loan from the bank, or I can't expand my business." In actuality, there are always three or more alternative solutions to any problem. Relax, brainstorm, and come up with as many alternative solutions as possible before discarding any possibilities as being unworkable.

After listing your alternatives, decide the advantages and disadvantages of each alternative. From this point, you can make your decision. Once you have made your decision, it is equally important to implement your decision and, after doing so, evaluate that decision. In this way, you can adjust the decision if need be and learn how to improve in making future decisions.

Decision-making Worksheet

Step One: State the problem in the form of a question.

Example: How can I get the machine I need to start my business?

Step Two: Gather and study pertinent information.

Step Three: Develop alternative solutions.

Alternative #1	Advantages	Disadvantages
Alternative #2		
Alternative #3		
Alternative #4		

Step Four: List the advantages and disadvantages of each.

Step Five: Select the best alternative.

Step Six: Implement the best decision.

Step Seven: Evaluate the decision.

Summing it up, individuals who are likely to be more successful than others in working from home:

- Like to work alone, enjoy solitude, and are able to structure their own time and use it effectively.

- Are willing to take calculated risks.

- Have the ability to approach tasks creatively.

- Are willing to work hard.

- Possess business knowledge or are willing to take the time to learn.

- Have good organizational skills.

- Are persevering and have stick-to-itiveness.

- Exhibit self-confidence and assertiveness in whatever they do.

- Are effective leaders who inspire loyalty.

- Possess strong management skills.

- Have a genuine interest in and concern for other people.

- Are willing to accept a great deal of responsibility.

- Like to set difficult goals and work to achieve them.

- Have the ability to make quick, accurate decisions.

- Are able to communicate clearly and persuasively.

If you feel you possess the above attributes and the idea of working from home sounds challenging and intriguing, a home business may be right for you.

Reasons for Working at Home

What is responsible for the current resurgence of interest in home-based businesses? Why are the 1990s expected to be a period of rapid growth in home enterprises? Clearly, there seem to be many advantages, both economic and personal, that help to explain why more and more people are choosing this mode of work.

Worker advantages

Even though the reasons for working from home are nearly as numerous as the types of people doing it, there are at least seven frequently cited reasons that people give for choosing the home as a workplace. More than in any other type of work, home workers are able to structure their own time and work environment so that they best suit their personal needs.

Economy. Financial advantages are often a major consideration. When compared with a traditional job at a centralized office, the home business person saves money on commuting, parking, lunches, child care, and an extensive work wardrobe. The home business person also saves money by not having to rent office space, pay for heating it, buy furnishings, and pay for maintenance. As fuel and office space continue to rise in cost, working from home becomes increasingly sound from an economic standpoint.

Time. Other advantages in working from home, while perhaps less tangible, are certainly just as important. By working from home, one saves time normally spent commuting. If a worksteader would normally spend thirty minutes driving to work, five hours a week would be saved by not commuting. That time can then be put to more advantageous use, either in the business or in some other area of a person's life.

Flexibility. Working from home allows for greater flexibility in working schedules than is generally found in traditional jobs. You can work early or late, take time out to pick up the children, or take care of other business or family obligations. Home-based work also allows for a better division of time between work and other activities. Home workers can arrange to have more time to spend with their spouses, children, and friends. Consequently, people who work in cottage industries often express the feeling that they have more control over their lives in general.

Special needs. Cottage industries are particularly beneficial for workers with special needs, such as mothers of young children, the disabled, students, and those caring for homebound individuals. Being able to work at home allows these people, who might otherwise be unable to enter the work force, to be gainfully employed. For some, the reason for working at home is quite simple. They are simply unable to work outside the home for either physical or family reasons. For these people, working at home may be not only the best but the only way to make a living.

In the recent past, working from home was often the only viable means of employment for the severely disabled. While some companies have increased opportunities for these workers, many disabled still choose to work at home. Technological developments, ranging from the commonplace telephone to sophisticated microcomputers, have opened up jobs to these people, enabling them to use their talents and abilities in spite of their disabilities. Microcomputers, particularly, have expanded opportunities for highly skilled jobs, allowing disabled people to lead much more independent lives.

Life-style. Worksteaders have the opportunity to engage in a more personally gratifying life-style, often being able to spend more time with their families. They can work independently, make their own decisions, and be their own bosses. And, since most worksteaders are working for themselves, they are often able to select work that they find personally satisfying and fulfilling.

Job satisfaction. Some people work at home running their own businesses as a way to get out of a dead-end job. Some express the desire for a change of occupation; others seek to supplement existing income. Some try a home business as a way to make money while pursuing a passion or hobby. Some operate businesses that keep them in contact with clients and keep their knowledge and skills abreast of what is happening in their particular field. This may be especially important for worksteaders who want to return later to traditional jobs.

Part-time work. Many people elect to work at home part-time. This may be in conjunction with their regular employment in a flexi-place arrangement, or it may be in addition to a regular job, to supplement existing income. Still others may only want to work part-time and find that running a business from home is the most rewarding part-time work available. In any of these three cases, home businesses are ideally suited because the individuals decide on the type of business and how much time they want to devote to it. The key here is the personal goal each individual has in mind.

Corporate advantages   Large companies make the decision to use home-based workers for quite different reasons from those influencing individual workers. Traditional businesses may become involved in the use of home work sites as a result of employee interest or to benefit from the business advantages of such arrangements. But in all cases, the continued success of commercial use of home workers depends on sound business considerations.

Greater productivity. Microcomputers and modems now make many jobs that previously were possible only in large offices with heavy mainframe computers not only possible but also economically profitable to be done in homes. Perhaps the most beneficial advantage for the employer is that telecommuting apparently results in greater productivity of workers. Telecommuting test programs carried out by numerous large companies showed that average productivity increased ten to twenty percent when employees worked from home. In some cases this figure was even higher.

Available workers. Another advantage for traditional employers is that they can hire people who might not otherwise be available for employment. By including those people outside the arena of traditional job seekers, a business considerably widens the pool from which it can draw employees. This is especially helpful if there is a shortage of skilled workers in a particular field.

Cost savings. Employers also benefit from saving the cost of office space as well as heating, cooling, and maintaining that office space. Using home-based workers can also lower the cost of computer time because home workers can use the computer during off-peak hours. Companies often find that home workers accomplish more work for each payroll dollar than traditional office workers, thus saving the business more money.

Health insurance and other employee benefits are a high cost item for businesses. In some cases, companies can save these costs by using home workers. Workers who are covered in other ways may not need these benefits and are willing to trade them off, in effect, for the greater freedom of working at home.

Advantages for society

In addition to the advantages for individual worksteaders and employers, home work also provides benefits to society at large. While several societal advantages are already apparent, as home work becomes more widespread, other benefits for our society will no doubt come to light.

Secure neighborhoods. In communities in which home work is prevalent, instances of crime have decreased, presumably because people around during the day discourage criminal activity such as theft. Knowing that there are adults present in the neighborhood may also discourage young people from engaging in pranks and vandalism. Thus, neighborhoods are more secure.

Reduced traffic. Since approximately twenty-three million people currently work from home, home workers greatly reduce the number of commuters on the highway. This results in reduced use of fuel, decreased air pollution, and less traffic congestion. Home work may also contribute to lower traffic accident rates by decreasing the amount of traffic. These effects are particularly significant because they affect peak commuting hours.

Closer family units. Another probable advantage for society is that home businesses allow families to spend a greater amount of time together, making parents available to their children on a more continuous basis. Parents in traditional jobs must depend on scarce day-care facilities or other child-care arrangements that often prove less than satisfactory. In contrast, child care usually presents fewer problems for home business people, since their work arrangements are more flexible. Thus, home-based work may prove to make for stronger, sounder family units.

Economic growth. Home businesses also contribute to the economic growth of our society. Although there are no accurate statistics currently available, home businesses clearly contribute to the gross national product and increase the country's tax base. Worksteaders, of course, spend their earnings to purchase other goods, which in turn contributes to the success of other businesses. In these ways home businesses do their share in promoting a healthy economy.

Disadvantages of Working at Home

Home workers are generally enthusiastic about working from home. They are quick to cite the advantages that home work has afforded them. Yet anyone who has worked from home could tell you that there are a number of problems as well.

While most of these problems can be alleviated or minimized, it's important for anyone contemplating working from home to consider the disadvantages as well as the advantages. After all, working at home isn't for everyone. However, since there are inherent problems in every type of work, the best approach is to look at potential areas of concern and determine honestly whether or not they are problems that you can deal with or overcome.

Isolation

Perhaps the biggest and most generally acknowledged problem is isolation. Many worksteaders work virtually alone. Even though home business people come in occasional contact with clients and customers, most of their working day is spent alone. When you work at home, you generally give up association with everyday colleagues.

Even if one is telecommuting and technically still has co-workers back at the office, isolation from these co-workers is likely to occur both during and outside business hours. Informal chats with co-workers no longer occur; and unfortunately, colleagues in the office often forget to include their telecommuting co-workers in social plans, such as impromptu gatherings after work.

An additional factor of isolation in home work is that a majority of contacts with others are likely to be by telephone, so home workers are likely to miss out on more personal face-to-face contact. This may be especially true for the telecommuter who has very little customer or client contact.

The single person, living and working alone, experiences different and potentially more severe problems. Coworkers, if there are any, may in effect become family to fill an emotional void. In light of medical research indicating that heart disease and high death rate are associated with social isolation, it is very important for the single worksteader to get out and see people regularly.

Home workers can do a number of simple things to alleviate feelings of isolation. Experienced cottage workers advise getting out of the house when you are not working. Keep up social contacts. Make plans for lunch with friends or clients. Get involved in hobbies or other interests which involve you with other people.

A second step that you can take is to arrange your work schedule so that your business takes you out of the house occasionally. Plan some meetings with your clients or other business contacts outside your home.

A third suggestion is to join professional and trade associations. Such associations, while getting you involved with other people with common interests, will also enable you to make new business contacts and to pick up ideas on how to improve your business. Thus, both you and your business may benefit.

Interruptions

Most types of work require an atmosphere that is relatively free of distractions and interruptions. While the traditional office setting is structured to keep interruptions of a social nature to a minimum, this is not always true of the home business setting. Interruptions can be a serious problem if there are children or other people around during your work hours.

In order to deal with the problem of interruptions, home workers should devise a system of letting friends and neighbors know when socializing, whether in person or by phone, is welcome and when it isn't. You need to help people learn to respect your working hours. As a home worker, you will have to resist the urge to visit or let family activities distract you from your work. When interruptions do bother you, remember that traditional offices aren't totally free from distractions either.

Family relationships

Another potential disadvantage of home business is that it may place a strain on family life. Working from home is unique in that no other working arrangement can have as much impact on relationships, both for those with families and for people living and working alone.

Worksteaders with families may find it quite difficult to avoid spillovers of business into family time and vice versa. When you work at home, it becomes difficult at times to leave your work at the end of a business day and to move into family activities. Conversely, crises in the home may have greater than usual effect on the worker's business life.

While being able to spend additional time with one's family may be desirable for some home workers, for others working while children and other family members are present may interfere greatly with work productivity. Many home business workers are stunned to find that their domestic roles as parents, wives, or husbands interfere significantly with their job efficiency.

Family members may become the primary social contacts in the work-at-home person's life, requiring emotional adjustments by all family members. While this may foster closer family bonds, it might also have the opposite effect of placing a strain on familial relationships. Many families are already snarled up in scheduling conflicts, trying to allocate limited time to competing activities. The introduction of work into the home life adds another layer of complexity and increases the potential for conflict. For many home business people, family members become closely involved in the business. While this can be good for family closeness, self-esteem, and esprit de corps, it may also place family members into employee-employer roles which can conflict with normal family relationships.

Dealing with these problems requires placing as much separation as possible between your working life and home life. One way to do this is to have fixed business hours, making it clear to family and friends that during those hours you are working.

A second step you can take is to have a separate phone for business. Then you can answer only your business phone while you are working and your family phone when you are not. In this way, business calls will not infringe on your family time, and people calling for other family members or for social reasons will not disrupt your work. An answering machine is another tool that can keep phone calls from being a disruption.

A third, very important step you can take to separate family and work is to place your work station in a relatively isolated part of the home. Having your office in a quiet bedroom or other seldom-used room will keep your business out of the family traffic flow. Further, both you and your family will come to associate that area with your work and will act accordingly when in that room.

Recognition as a serious business

Another potential problem for home workers is being recognized and respected as a serious business. In our society, fair or not, much of a person's worth is viewed in terms of one's job. Much of our self-esteem is an outgrowth of the idea that our work is important or has something to contribute to the world at large. The value that family and friends place on your work may influence your success in working from home. Business contacts may not take you seriously at first when they learn you work at home.

The most important factor in combating this problem is for you to take your home business seriously. Show others that your work is a legitimate, professional business by your own example. Keep regular business hours. Present a professional image and always conduct business in a professional, ethical manner. Follow through on your business claims; deliver whatever you promise clients. And finally, operate strictly "above ground." Nothing legitimizes a business more quickly than the fact that it is run absolutely legitimately.

Independence and flexibility as drawbacks

Independence and flexibility, two frequently cited advantages to working from home, can just as easily be viewed as problems by some people. While working independently may be a boon to some workers, it may be a burden for others. Independence puts more pressure on the individual to structure time and to use it effectively.

People may have to make substantial adjustments to cope with a home work environment. Home presents temptations of television, the refrigerator, or the easy chair in the corner. In contrast, a traditional office atmosphere is marked by the presence of managers and office routines that put structure into the worker's day that is not readily present at home.

Central to working independently is the ability to organize one's time and use it well. Often it is difficult to discipline yourself into working when you just don't feel like it.

The other side of the coin is overextending yourself. Home businesses often require that one person fulfill many different job roles. Overcommitting time or trying to do too much are pitfalls that can be very stressful. When you work at home, you must learn to pace your own work. Home business people must possess or develop self-discipline as well as the ability to keep a balance in their lives.

We have already discussed the types of people likely to be successful in working from home. Now, having examined some of the problems associated with home work, you should be better able to decide whether or not home work is suitable for you.

Home-based Business Pros and Cons

Each person has different goals and needs. Weigh your home business decision by listing the pros and cons of a home-based business as it pertains to your own life. We've started each list for you.

Pros	Cons
Lower cost for office space	Zoning and other restrictions
Lower start-up costs	Isolation
Lower fixed costs	Space limitations
Tax benefits	Security concerns
Flexible life-style	Separation from home life
No commuting	

_____   _____

_____   _____

_____   _____

_____   _____

_____   _____

_____   _____

_____   _____

Frank Schiff, vice-president and chief economist of the Committee for Economic Development summarizes in the article "Flexiplace: An Idea Whose Time Has Come" the issues involved when he says, "More flexibility in workplace arrangements can benefit *particular* people in *particular* circumstances and at *particular* times in their careers." Know yourself, know the work you want to do, and decide what is right for you.

Educational Preparation

Since cottage industries include many different types of work, there is no one ideal educational background for working from home. In home business, educational needs vary depending on the type of business chosen.

Clearly, a person running a word processing service and a person operating a law practice from home would require completely different educational backgrounds. Nonetheless, there are similarities that most home businesses share; consequently, knowledge in these areas is important for all entrepreneurs.

Generally speaking, whatever educational preparation is required to obtain work in a particular field in the traditional job force will also be necessary to run that same business from home. Thus, an individual planning to operate a real estate office from home would need to study the course work and pass whatever exams are necessary for real estate agents in a given state. Working from home is not a shortcut around usual requirements for a job. In fact, more skill and knowledge are often required to run one's own business than to work for someone else.

In most cottage industries, business knowledge is of great importance. If one's background is in some area other than business, it would probably be advantageous to take one or more courses to learn the fundamentals of business.

My Experience and Education

1. What kinds of job experiences and/or volunteer experiences do you have? _____

   _____

   _____

2. What skills have you learned from your work experiences? _____

   _____

   _____

3. Have you had any experience in running a business? _____

   _____

4. Have you ever been a manager? _____

   _____

5. Do you know how to set up and operate a record-keeping system? _____

   _____

6. What other types of business knowledge do you possess? _____

   _____

   _____

7. What formal education have you had? _____

   _____

   _____

8. What things have you learned from your educational experiences that could help you in a home business?

   _____

   _____

   _____

Various individuals, organizations, and vocational and technical schools offer courses, workshops, and seminars geared to starting or improving small businesses. For practical purposes, nearly all information about small business also pertains to home business. While most business courses will provide useful information to the home business person, specific training for home businesses is also often available.

Another good source of workshops and other information on home businesses are University Small Business Development Centers. Usually set up as a community outreach activity, these centers offer seminars and other information on running small businesses.

There are also numerous newsletters and a variety of books which are specifically geared to working from home. The Appendix contains recommended readings with information for home-based entrepreneurs.

The U.S. Small Business Administration (SBA) has offices all over the country, and its primary purpose is to help individuals who run small businesses or who would like to start a small business. In addition to seminars and workshops, the SBA has an abundance of literature available on topics important to home business people. Business experts are on staff to offer advice on your small business problems, and they can also help you locate other sources of information available in your area.

Selecting a Home Business

In a home business, as with any type of enterprise, it's of great importance to research the business thoroughly before you begin. Big companies are continuously doing market research and surveys to keep aware of their customers' wants and needs. They field-test before launching products to make sure that they will have a viable market. These companies are successful, in part, because they realize that you have to know your market in order to develop a product or service that you can be reasonably certain people will buy.

Selecting Your Business

Unfortunately, many people enter a home business blindly, deciding on a product or service that may or may not sell in their area. And all too many people start home businesses without doing any research on what it really takes to run a business. Lacking vital information about bookkeeping, taxes, zoning laws, marketing, and other areas vital to a successful business, these would-be entrepreneurs often doom their businesses to failure before they even begin.

Clearly, having an abundance of the right kind of information is essential to starting and running a successful cottage industry. When researching, planning, and organizing a home business, it's a good idea to actually write down every aspect of your study and preparation.

Analyze yourself More than in any other type of business, you are the most important influence on the success or failure of your home business. So it is important to analyze yourself first. Decide what your special talents and abilities are. Your strong points might include special talents or skills, enthusiasm, past experience, or the ability to think logically. Write down anything you think could be an asset for your home business.

Then take a look at your weaknesses or problem areas. Everyone has areas of comparative weakness, but it's important for you to recognize exactly where your problem areas lie. Do you love big ideas but hate details? Do you have trouble keeping yourself on a schedule? Is it difficult for you to write well? Is your tolerance for frustration limited? It's only after recognizing your weak spots that you can do anything to counter them.

Assess your long- and short-term goals, both personal and business. What type of business do you envision yourself running? How large do you want your business to be, both in terms of number of employees and volume of business? Realistically, what level of income do you expect your business to generate in its first year? What income do you expect it to generate in successive years? How much time do you want to devote to your business? Specifically, what type of personal life-style are you striving to obtain? Can you satisfy your family obligations and other responsibilities adequately, particularly while extending yourself during the early stages of developing your business?

It's very possible that not all of your goals can be met. Some may be mutually contradictory. It may be, for example, that more time is likely to be necessary in the initial stages of your business than you would like, reducing time with your family. Or you may have to accept the likelihood that, initially, low income will require that you perform business tasks you dislike, such as bookkeeping, which you would rather hire someone else to do.

Compromises between conflicting goals will probably be necessary. Only you can decide what compromises you are willing and able to make in order to initiate or expand your business. Are you willing to earn less money if you can do work you particularly enjoy? Perhaps you wouldn't mind working weekends if you could end workdays early during the week. Knowing what compromises you are not willing to make is just as important, so take them into consideration as well.

Analyze Yourself

Special Talents and Abilities

List your special talents, skills, and abilities. For each one, note how it could be an asset to a business.

_____

_____

_____

_____

_____

Weaknesses or Problem Areas

List your personal weaknesses or problem areas. For each one, list one or more ways to fix or work around the problem.

_____

_____

_____

_____

_____

Short Term Goals

Personal—How do you envision your life by this time next year? In three years? What will your life-style be like?

_____

_____

_____

_____

Business—Specifically, what type(s) of business do you want to run? What goals do you have for your business in the first year? In three years?

_____

_____

_____

_____

_____

Long Term Goals

Personal—What are your personal goals for the next five years? For the next ten years?

_____

_____

_____

_____

Business—What are your business goals for the next five years? For the next ten years? How much business do you plan to be doing? How do you envision your business changing?

_____

_____

_____

_____

Analyze your market   After analyzing yourself and coming to understand the strengths and weaknesses you bring to a business, you are ready to analyze your business opportunities. In essence, what needs to be accomplished in this step is to research market needs, which can then be translated into business opportunities.

First, analyze the population in your target market area. Look at demographic details such as age, average income, geographic location, and prevalent life-styles. Life-styles include such things as work, transportation, family size and structure, as well as leisure activities. This population comprises your potential customers, so it's important to know about them, at least in a general sense.

In looking at the life-styles of the people in your area, certain needs should become apparent. For example, if nearly all of the women work and there is a large elderly population, both working women and the elderly have special needs. Pinpoint exactly what these needs are. Then look at how these needs are currently being met. Are they being met adequately? In what manner? Is there a demand for a service or a product to answer these particular needs?

Having defined these needs, decide what products or services can meet them. Ask yourself the following questions:

- What or where is the market?

- What is the size of the market?

- Who is presently servicing that market?

Based on the answers to these questions, you should be able to select the products and/or services that are in the greatest demand and that you want to provide. Base your decision on market size and need rather than on personal preference. You may love to crochet heirloom lace, but if there is no market for lace in your area and you can't locate a market for it, it would not be wise to base a business on such a product.

Analyze Your Market

Analyze the Population

List demographics for your target market area. Specifically address age, income level, marital status, family size, employment status, types of employment, and special information that pertains to your possible business.

_____

_____

_____

_____

Analyze Market Needs

List several needs that have become apparent from your research.

_____

_____

_____

_____

For each need, answer the following questions:

Are these needs being met? How? _____

_____

_____

Are current services/products adequate or inadequate to meet the need?

_____

_____

Is there demand for a service or product to answer this particular need?

_____

_____

What new (or existing) products or services would answer this need? _____

_____

_____

Writing Your Business Plan

Having decided on a product or service, you now need to research and write your business plan. While it may seem tedious or time consuming, don't shortchange this important step. Your business plan should be detailed and well thought out before you actually start running your business. A good business plan can help you to organize every aspect of your business and can even help to avoid problems before they arise. Should you need a loan or investors for start-up capital, a well-thought-out business plan is an invaluable tool to present to bankers or potential investors.

A business plan outline is included here. You will no doubt have to read subsequent sections of this book, do additional research, and consult various experts in order to complete the various sections of the business plan. Other worksheets have also been provided that will help you to complete some sections of your business plan. Some will actually be included as part of your business plan. For this reason, it would be wise to read through this book before attempting to complete the entire business plan.

Sample Business Plan

1. **Name of Firm.** State legal name of the business.

_____

2. **Owner(s).**   State names of owner(s) and the form and percent of ownership in the case of a partnership or other shared ownership plan.

_____

_____

_____

3. **Type of Business.**   State the nature of the business (e.g., retail flower shop).

_____

_____

4. **Goals of the Business.**   State the goals of the business in terms of the specific services or products you will offer.

_____

_____

_____

_____

5. **Workplace.**   State the address and a description of the workplace. Is the site rented, owned, or leased, from whom and under what conditions? State intended hours of operation.

_____

_____

_____

_____

6. **Personnel.**   If applicable, state the number of employees you will need, the training they will be expected to have, and the availability of such workers.

_____

_____

_____

_____

7. **Economic Projections.**   Describe how this business will make money. State how prices will be determined. State what financial records will be kept and by whom.

_____

_____

_____

_____

8. **Inventory and Supplies.**   State what inventory, materials, or supplies the business will need initially and in the future. List your suppliers. Determine the costs of maintaining adequate supplies. Identify any problems you anticipate in securing supplies, for example, scarcity or fluctuating prices.

_____

_____

_____

_____

9. **Legal Definition of the Business.**   State the legal form of the business (sole proprietorship, partnership, corporation, or subchapter S corporation). Identify the insurance, zoning, or licensing requirements that may affect the business. Describe how you will comply with any applicable building and health codes.

_____

_____

_____

_____

10. **Future Plans.**   State what you anticipate your business will be in one year, three years, and five years. Do you plan to expand, maintain, diversify, or sell the business?

_____

_____

_____

_____

11. **Market Study.**   Define exactly who your customers will be. (Use the separate worksheet on Market Study.)

12. **Market Strategy.**   Describe how you will sell your product or service, how you will get customers, and how you will deliver or distribute your service or product. Describe your plan of action for marketing: advertising in newspapers, telephone solicitation, word of mouth, professional associations or, for example, direct-mail advertising. (Use Market Strategy and Market Plan worksheets.)

13. **Competition.**   Identify your most important competitors. Describe how your business will be better than theirs. Discuss how your product or service meets market needs and how you compare with the competition in terms of price, location, service features, reliability, and other factors. (Use Competition Analysis worksheet for this section.)

14. **Management.** Describe who will make what key decisions. If you are entering a partnership with one or more people, write up an agreement stating your intentions and describing arrangements if a partner wishes to withdraw at a later date. Identify the business and management experience that you and your partners have. State how much time you will devote to operating the business. Discuss local contacts or trade associations that may be helpful. Identify expert advisors you will look to for help: an attorney, an accountant, a consultant, a mentor.

_____

_____

_____

_____

_____

_____

15. **Financial Information.**   Describe the cash assets that you will need to get started. Detail the way the money will be used. Describe what you will need and for what you will use it. List projected sources of money for the project. Prepare detailed financial projections that describe:

- Source and application of funding—where you plan to get the money you need and how it will be used.

_____

_____

_____

_____

_____

- Projected profit and loss statement, detailed in the first year and more general for the two years following. (Use the Projected Profits and Losses worksheet.)

- Projected cash flow—a monthly forecast of what cash will come into the business and what will go out. (Use the Projected Cash Flow worksheet.)

- Projected balance sheets—what the business owns and what liabilities it will have. (Use the provided Balance Sheet.)

Planning Resources   All stages of planning a business require resources of reliable information. The following list will give you some sources of information to help research the many facets of your business plan.

Key Resources for Writing Your Business Plan

You may find these general resources useful in planning your business:
Bankers
Chamber of Commerce
Community College Small Business Center
Cooperative Extension Services
Department of Commerce and Community Affairs
Libraries and reference librarians
Trade associations
Utility companies
Wholesalers and other suppliers

These are questions you will need to answer and sources you can consult to find the appropriate information:
- Characteristics of the population—Age? Sex? Income? Education? Occupation?
- What geographic area will your market cover?

Sources:
Census information (library)
Utility companies' community profiles
Department of Commerce and Community Affairs' community profiles
County business pattern (library)
Survey of buying power

- What is the population of the market? (current figures, projected growth, and any other expected changes)
- What portion of population is seasonal?

Sources:
Market Statistics Sales and Marketing Management 1986 "Survey of Buying Power"
1987 Rand McNally Commercial Atlas and Marketing Guide
State Department of Tourism
Chamber of Commerce

- What are the development plans for the area? Will plans change flow of traffic or shopping patterns? What business and/or residential development is planned?

Sources:
City and/or county planners
Industrial development groups
Chamber of Commerce

- How much money is being spent in the market area for the potential product or service?

Sources:
1986 "Survey of Buying Power"
Census of service industries
Census of retail trade
Trade associations

- What are the major trends in the industry? Now? In five years? In ten years?

Sources:
U.S. Industrial Outlook
Trade association information (Found in the *Encyclopedia of Associations*)
Wholesalers or manufacturers

Market Study
(Section 11 of the Business Plan)

1. Your customers are your market. Show who your customers are: wholesalers, retailers, consumers, public entities.

_____

_____

_____

_____

2. List the characteristics of your customers: age, location, life-styles, income range, and other pertinent information. The more information you have about your market, the better you can sell your service or product.

_____

_____

_____

_____

3. Describe why your product or service is needed.

_____

_____

_____

_____

4. Determine what your customers will like about your product or service.

_____

_____

_____

_____

5. Describe what you will do to attract and keep customers.

_____

_____

_____

_____

Marketing Strategy
(Section 12 of the Business Plan)

How will customers be attracted? _____

_____

_____

_____

How will prices be determined and by whom? _____

_____

_____

_____

What special sales terms will be offered? _____

_____

_____

_____

What method of selling, distributing, and servicing will be used? _____

_____

_____

_____

What types of advertising and sales promotion will be most effective to reach your market? _____

_____

_____

_____

What will the advertising cost be? _____

_____

_____

_____

Market Plan
(Sections 12 and 13 of the Business Plan)

Who is your market?

• Describe the profile of your typical customer.

Ages: _____

Male, female, both: _____

Average family size: _____

Annual family income: _____

Location: _____

Buying patterns: _____

Reason to buy from you: _____

Other: _____

• Geographically describe your trading area.

Is it the city, county, state, nation? _____

_____

(You may want to outline the area on a map.)

• Economically describe your trading area. (single/family, average earnings, number of children)

_____

How large is the market?

Total units or dollars: _____

Growing _____ Steady _____ Decreasing _____

If growing, annual growth rate: _____

Who is your competition?

Direct competitors (names and addresses): _____

_____

_____

Similar or marginally competitive businesses: _____

_____

_____

Which are the closest ones? _____

_____

_____

How are their businesses similar to or competitive with yours?

_____

_____

_____

Do you have a unique niche? Describe it. _____

_____

_____

How will your service or product be better or more saleable than that of your competitors? _____

_____

_____

Are their businesses growing? Stable? Declining? Why? _____

_____

_____

What can be learned from observing their operations and/or talking to their present or former clients?

_____

_____

Will you have competitive advantages, disadvantages, or both by operating from home? Be honest.

_____

_____

What will be your market share?

Market share is the allocation of total sales of "like" businesses. You can roughly calculate the minimum population needed to support a business like yours by checking the yellow pages to find similar businesses in your area, then using this formula:

$$\frac{\text{Total population}}{\text{Number of businesses}} = \text{Minimum population}$$

Competition Analysis Worksheet
(Section 13 of the Business Plan)

Competitor				
Address				
Reputation				
Strengths/ Weaknesses				
Pricing Policies				
Advertising and Public Relations				
Strategies for Competition				

Legal Considerations

Many aspects of business are regulated by the laws and regulations of various levels of government. As such, these legal considerations provide the basic framework for a business. While there are numerous laws and regulations concerned with running a business, the major areas to be considered include the legal structure or type of business organization, licensing and zoning laws, and state and federal regulations related to your particular type of business and to home businesses in general. Let's briefly examine each of these areas.

Legal structure

Perhaps the most basic legal consideration in beginning a home business is deciding which legal structure is most appropriate for your business. The legal structure of a business affects how you and any partners are paid, how profits are treated, and how you will pay taxes on your business.

There is no one best structure for a home-based business, since different businesses have different needs. The brief summary of structures that follows is not meant to substitute for specific, in-depth study of your own business and personal financial situation. Talking with an attorney about your particular business should help you decide which is best for you.

Basically, there are four types of business structures. Each one has advantages and disadvantages, so it's important to select a structure which is most appropriate for your own situation.

Sole Proprietorship. Perhaps the most common type of business structure among small home enterprises is the sole proprietorship. In a sole proprietorship, one person (or one person and spouse) goes into business without formalizing the structure. A sole proprietor does not pay her- or himself wages. The profit or loss of the business is considered to be the owner's earnings. A sole proprietor's earnings are subject to self-employment tax.

The main advantage of the sole proprietorship is that it is the simplest form of business. Comparatively, a sole proprietorship requires very little record keeping; all that it requires are a simple bookkeeping system and a bank account. For a person inexperienced in running a business, the tax rules and other legal ramifications of this business structure are the most straightforward and the easiest to learn and comprehend.

A major disadvantage of the sole proprietorship is that

the owner of such a business is personally liable for the debts of the company. If the business should have financial problems, the owner's personal assets are at risk in addition to the assets of the business. The owner's personal assets are also vulnerable if a lawsuit is filed against the business, although insurance can help to protect the owner in such an instance.

Partnership. A partnership is formed when two or more individuals decide to operate a business and don't elect to incorporate. A partnership may or may not have a formal written partnership agreement. All partners are liable for the debts of a partnership, and the profit or loss of the enterprise is divided among the partners. If there is a written agreement (which we strongly recommend), the profit or loss is divided according to the agreement. Otherwise the profit or loss is divided equally among the partners.

The partnership files an informational Form 1065 with the Internal Revenue Service but does not pay taxes per se. The partners each pay taxes on their share of the profit or loss. Usually, income from a partnership is subject to self-employment tax.

Like the sole proprietorship, a partnership is a relatively simple legal structure. The advantages of a partnership relate to having a partner. Responsibility for the business can be divided among the partners. Presumably each partner brings different talents and skills to the business. Another important consideration is that, financially, it may be easier for a partnership rather than one person to raise start-up capital.

One disadvantage of a partnership is that it requires more documentation than a sole proprietorship. Another disadvantage of a partnership is that disagreements or problems can occur between partners, sometimes to the point of endangering the business. For this reason it is imperative that partners discuss the division of profits and potential problems and their solutions and that they form a written partnership agreement.

Corporation. A corporation is a formal, highly regulated enterprise that is a separate legal entity, franchised by a state. It is a business owned by shareholders and operated for the benefit of these shareholders.

A corporation pays taxes on its profits at corporate rates. Shareholders report only the income they receive from the corporation, either as a salary or as dividends.

The corporation is liable for the business debts of the enterprise, while the shareholders are not. So shareholders can only lose the amount of money that they have invested or loaned to a corporation.

The major advantage of a corporation is that it is a separate legal entity. Consequently, personal assets are protected if the business has financial problems. Historically there have also been a number of tax benefits for corporations, such as reduced tax rates on corporate profits. Some changes in that situation have been proposed, and new legislation may affect the traditional tax structures soon.

The biggest disadvantage of a corporation is that it is an extremely complex legal structure, requiring a great deal of accounting and legal expertise. Setting up a corporation entails a considerable amount of formal paperwork and expense that is not necessary for sole proprietorships and partnerships. For most home businesses, incorporation is not a practical or advantageous alternative, although there are exceptions.

Subchapter S corporation. A subchapter S corporation is a corporation which is eligible to and elects to be taxed in the same manner as a partnership. The individual owners, then, report the profit or loss on their individual tax returns.

A subchapter S corporation must also file a tax form 1120S and pay taxes on investment earnings of the corporation, but the form 1120S passes loss as well as profit through to the shareholders. Like a corporation, the subchapter S corporation pays salaries to its employee-owners, so income of the owners is not subject to self-employment tax.

This legal structure is somewhat of a hybrid between unincorporated and incorporated structures of business, having some of the advantages and disadvantages of each. One advantage of the subchapter S corporation is that it is a separate legal entity, affording its owners protection of personal assets. Another advantage is that earnings are not subject to self-employment tax.

Since the subchapter S corporation is taxed in the same manner as a partnership, the tax advantages normally associated with a corporation may not be applicable. And unlike a corporation, company losses are passed on to the owners. Recent changes in tax laws have given some new tax advantages to subchapter S corporations.

Remember that the ramifications of these legal structures may change from time to time, and the most advantageous legal structure varies according to individual business needs. Secure up-to-date information and advice from reliable sources.

Business legal structures at a glance

Sole Proprietorship

1. The business is simple to organize.
2. The owner has maximum freedom to make decisions.
3. The business has a minimum of legal restrictions.
4. The owner receives all the profits.
5. The business is easy to discontinue.

Disadvantages

1. The owner has unlimited liability and risks all assets including personal assets not used in the business.
2. There is a limited ability to raise capital.

Partnership

1. It is easy to organize.
2. It may have greater financial strength than a sole proprietorship.
3. It combines managerial skills and judgments of the partners.
4. It has a definite legal status.
5. Each partner has a personal interest in the business.

Disadvantages

1. Liability of the partner is usually unlimited. Each partner may be held liable for all the debts of the business.
2. The authority for decisions is divided. Disputes may disrupt the business.

Corporation

1. The life of the business is perpetual.
2. The stockholders have limited liability.
3. Transfer of ownership is easy.
4. It is easier for corporations to raise capital and to expand than it is for other forms of business.

5. Management is generally more efficient.
6. It is adaptable to both small and large businesses.

Disadvantages

1. It is subject to special taxation.
2. It is more difficult and expensive to organize.
3. The corporate charter restricts the types of business activities.

Subchapter S Corporation

1. It is a corporation which is taxed in the same way as a partnership.
2. As a separate legal entity, it protects the owners' personal assets.
3. Earnings are not subject to self-employment tax.
4. New tax laws provide additional tax benefits.

Disadvantages

1. Losses as well as profits are passed on to the owners.
2. Tax benefits normally associated with corporations may not apply.
3. It is more complex to organize than a sole proprietorship or partnership.

Licensing and zoning laws

Zoning laws are generally the biggest obstacles entrepreneurs face in trying to operate legally from home. Regulations vary widely; but in general, there are more restrictions if the business is a retail trade, engages in outside advertising, or employs people outside of the household. Zoning laws are used to protect neighborhoods from intrusive businesses.

When considering a home business, you need to know what the zoning laws are in your neighborhood. Zoning laws vary from community to community and usually can be checked by contacting your local city hall and requesting the zoning ordinances for your area. Some communities have booklets regarding their zoning regulations that can be purchased for a nominal fee. Zoning ordinances will usually also address issues such as traffic, noise levels, number of workers, parking restrictions, and delivery restrictions. If not, other city ordinances will no doubt address such issues, so make sure you are in compliance with these ordinances as well.

If your neighborhood is zoned both residential and commercial, you should have no problem conducting your business from home. Many communities require only that you fill out a form describing certain aspects of your business and pay a yearly licensing fee registering your business with the city.

Even if your neighborhood is zoned residential, this does not necessarily preclude your operating a low-profile business from your home. Some municipalities make provisions in their zoning ordinances to allow low-profile home businesses in residentially zoned areas. Even if your particular city doesn't normally allow this, it is often possible to get a variance in order to run a business from your home in a residential zone. Usually you must show that your business will not be a disruption to your neighbors by fostering undue traffic or causing excessive noise.

While it is certainly understandable that most of us would not want to live next door to an all-night car repair shop, most home businesses are barely visible and present little or no disturbance to their neighbors. Being a good neighbor is essential to the success of your business.

Since zoning laws and regulations on home businesses vary widely from community to community, it's important for you to check the regulations of your own community before moving ahead on home business plans. Don't depend on what someone from a nearby community tells you, since regulations in your city could be completely different. No doubt as home businesses become more common, zoning laws will be changed to accommodate them. But until then you will have to deal with the zoning laws in your community as best you can.

Licenses   Many types of businesses are required by law to have a license or permit in order to operate. Businesses may be regulated and licensed by different departments of the federal, state, city, county, town, or village government. Which particular businesses require licenses varies from state to state and even from city to city. You can check with your local Chamber of Commerce or your city or county government, or you can consult your attorney in order to determine whether or not your business requires a license or permit.

Some businesses that commonly require licensing include real estate agencies, day-care centers, hairdressers and barbers, food stores, all types of eating establishments, vendors, peddlers and solicitors, taxi services, and upholsterers. This list is not exhaustive by any means, so you should determine the need to license any business before you begin. Requirements and procedures for obtaining necessary licenses and permits vary depending on the state and city in which you live. A telephone call to city or county officials should provide you with this information, plus advice on any health, safety, and labor laws that might apply to your undertaking.

In addition to licenses for specific types of business, your city may require that you register your home business with the city and pay a nominal licensing or registration fee, regardless of the type of business you intend to operate. The purpose of this type of licensing is basically to keep the city in control of the businesses in its area. Usually you will have to fill out a form that asks questions about the type of business being operated, traffic and parking concerns, provisions for waste disposal, size of business, and assets held by the business.

As long as your enterprise is not a disruptive influence in your neighborhood, you will most likely be allowed to proceed with the operation of your business. You can check with your attorney or local government representative to determine what other paperwork, if any, is necessary in order to run a business in your area.

State and federal regulations

Other legal issues that you must take into consideration are state and federal regulations regarding home businesses. As with zoning ordinances, state regulations on home businesses vary from state to state. Your state may or may not have laws which relate specifically to home work. New Jersey is one of eighteen states that has its own anti-home work regulations.

In order to gain information regarding home business regulations in your state, you can contact your state department of Industry, Labor, and Human Relations. Check the Appendix for sources of basic guidelines on state home business laws.

When checking into state laws governing home business, be sure also to check on regulations concerning the particular type of business you wish to enter. For example, if you want to run a cake decorating service, you should check regulations concerning health, safety, and food services, as well as regulations which specifically address home businesses, since any health and food regulations will also pertain to your enterprise.

Some federal regulations also exist regarding certain types of home businesses. The Industrial Home Work Act of 1943 banned seven specific areas of business from being conducted from the home. These included manufacture of buttons and buckles, embroidery, gloves and mittens, knitted outerwear, handkerchiefs, jewelry, and women's clothing. Several years ago the ban against home manufacture of knitted outerwear was fought and lifted, paving the way to lift the ban on the other six areas of industry. While this ban against home manufacturing in these areas has been lifted as of January 1989, several unions have filed suit to reinstate the ban. This legislation continues to be a source of controversy, and the eventual outcome is uncertain. If you want to produce items in any of the above areas, be sure to check on the status of this Act before proceeding.

When you seek legal advice about your business structure, have your attorney check out other pertinent government regulations as well. The local office of the Small Business Administration can provide you with a wealth of information about federal regulations and taxes, and you should take advantage of their help and advice.

What Laws Apply to My Business?

Find out which laws will affect your particular business. Be sure to jot down things you will need to do or remember.

Yes **No**

_____ _____ 1. County or city zoning restrictions.

_____

_____

_____ _____ 2. Permits and licenses necessary for operation.

_____

_____

_____ _____ 3. Local, state, and federal laws affecting home business.

_____

_____

_____ _____ 4. Regulations regarding parking, customer access, and deliveries.

_____

_____

_____ _____ 5. Sanitation, traffic, and noise codes.

_____

_____

_____ _____ 6. Restrictions on signs and advertising.

_____

_____

_____ _____ 7. State and federal code requirements for space, ventilation, heat, and light.

_____

_____

_____ _____ 8. Limitations on number and type of workers allowed in a home business.

_____

_____

_____ _____ 9. Deed or lease restrictions as to use of property; covenants and restrictive conditions of purchase.

_____

_____

_____ _____ 10. State laws pertaining to the specific business being considered.

_____

_____

Setting Up Business: Financial Issues

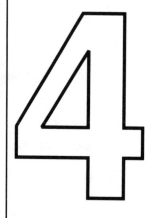

Starting any type of business requires a certain amount of investment capital. Running a business demands that operating expenses be met. And, ultimately, the goal of any business is to earn wages for its employees and produce a profit for its owner. Financial matters, then, play an integral role in the start-up and operation of every business.

Careful consideration of money matters is important in every stage of business operation. If you are casual or careless in handling financial aspects of a business, you greatly reduce your chances of showing a profit. You may even threaten the very existence of your business. Conversely, good financial planning and careful money management will put your business on the road to success.

Planning a Budget   One of the most prevalent causes for the failure of new businesses is undercapitalization. A rule of thumb is to have enough capital on hand to pay all expenses for at least a year, even if you don't take in a cent of business. Most small businesses take a year to reach the break-even point and don't start showing a profit until later. Your home business may start making money sooner, however, simply because you won't have the largest single expense of most businesses—rent.

Even conscientious people who try to plan for a year often overlook a number of expenses. Be sure your projected expenses include such items as utilities, telephone bill, license fees, taxes, social security payments, and payment of income taxes on estimated income.

If you have employees, you must also budget for workmen's compensation and unemployment insurance. Liability insurance coverage can be a major expense that you may overlook. Your capital must also be large enough to cover supplies and materials you will need even if your customers are slow in paying their bills.

Not all expenses fall due every month. Your projected budget should include the amounts you need to set aside each month to pay major expenses such as quarterly insurance premiums and taxes when they fall due. Otherwise, you may suddenly find that three or four major bills are pending at the same time, and it will look like your business is going under. Work out your budgeting so that you anticipate such expenses.

How Much Money Do You Need?

One-Time Start-Up Costs:

Fixtures and equipment   _____

Decorating and remodeling   _____

Installation of equipment   _____

Starting inventory   _____

Deposits with utilities   _____

Legal and professional fees   _____

Licenses and permits   _____

Initial advertising costs   _____

Cash   _____

Other _____   _____

_____   _____

_____   _____

                    TOTAL   _____

Monthly Expenses

Draw (if applicable)   _____

Salaries and wages   _____

Rent (if applicable)   _____

Advertising   _____

Delivery expenses   _____

Supplies   _____

Telephone   _____

Utilities   _____

Insurance   _____

Taxes, including Social Security   _____

Loan and interest payments   _____

Maintenance   _____

Legal and professional fees   _____

Miscellaneous   _____

                    TOTAL   _____
                                    <u>X12</u>

            TOTAL YEARLY EXPENSES_____

            + TOTAL ONE-TIME COSTS_____

                    TOTAL CASH NEEDED_____

Assets and Liabilities   Having planned a preliminary budget, it is important to determine your personal assets and liabilities. Since it is likely that you will be financing all or part of your business start-up, you need to have some knowledge of your net worth so that you have an accurate picture of the personal resources you have to devote to your home business.

First, take stock of your assets. Anything you own that has monetary value can be considered an asset. Cash, savings accounts, investment accounts, equity in your home, real estate, and stocks and bonds are among the most common assets you might have. Other assets you should not overlook include whole life insurance, pension plans, retirement accounts, and loans you have made to other people. If you already own some of the equipment, furnishings, or supplies you will need to run your business, consider these as assets too.

Next, list your liabilities. A liability can be defined as anything you owe. Your liabilities might include bank loans, personal loans, and payments left on your car, furnishings, or appliances. Other types of liabilities you should consider are taxes that have not yet been paid, outstanding bills, and the amount left on a mortgage. Monthly living expenses should not be included as liabilities, although you should allow for them in any budget you plan.

After you have totalled your assets and liabilities, you can easily determine your net worth. Simply subtract your total liabilities from your total assets. The resulting figure is your net worth. Your net worth should give you a realistic picture of your financial status and the amount of personal capital you can afford to invest in your business. When determining how much money you can put toward your business, remember that some of your assets are inaccessible, either because they represent necessities your family cannot do without or because they are not easily liquidated.

Another approach you can take is to figure your current yearly income and your yearly living expenses. Knowing these figures will help you determine how much of your total income you can afford to invest in your business. If you plan on drawing part or all of your living expenses from the proceeds of your business, figuring your current living expenses will give you an indication of the volume of business you will need to do.

Personal Net Worth Statement

Year _____

Assets	**Liabilities**
Cash	Unpaid Bills
On hand _____	Taxes _____
Checking accounts _____	Insurance premiums _____
Savings accounts _____	Charge accounts _____
Money owed me _____	Other unpaid bills _____
Investments	Installment Loans
Savings bonds _____	Automobile _____
Stocks and bonds _____	Other _____
Mutual funds _____	_____
Other _____	Loans
Cash value	Bank _____
Life insurance _____	Education _____
Annuities _____	Home equity _____
Pension fund _____	Other _____
Real estate _____	Mortgage loans
Personal property _____	Home _____
Automobiles _____	Other _____
Other assets:	Other liabilities:
_____	_____
_____	_____
TOTAL ASSETS _____	_____
	TOTAL LIABILITIES _____
	TOTAL ASSETS _____
	–TOTAL LIABILITIES _____
	TOTAL NET WORTH _____

Personal Income Statement

Year _____

Income

Husband   _____

Wife   _____

Wages or salary   _____

Dividends and interest   _____

Capital gains and losses   _____

Rents, annuities, pensions   _____

Other _____   _____

TOTAL INCOME   _____

Taxes

Personal income taxes   _____

Social Security taxes   _____
                                              –

TOTAL TAXES   _____

AMOUNT REMAINING FOR LIVING EXPENSES AND INVESTMENT   _____

Living Expenses	*Fixed*	or	*Variable*
Housing			
Rent or mortgage	_____		_____
Utilities	_____		_____
Insurance	_____		_____
Taxes	_____		_____
Maintenance/repairs	_____		_____
Other _____	_____		_____

Food   _____   _____

Clothing   _____   _____

Transportation

   Gas   _____   _____

   Repairs   _____   _____

   Licenses and fees   _____   _____

   Insurance   _____   _____

   Auto payments or purchase   _____   _____

   Other   _____   _____

Recreation, entertainment,
and vacations   _____   _____

Medical

   Doctor(s)   _____   _____

   Dentist(s)   _____   _____

   Medicines   _____   _____

   Insurance   _____   _____

   Hospital   _____   _____

   Other expenses   _____   _____

Personal   _____   _____

Life insurance   _____   _____

Other expenses

_____   _____   _____

_____   _____   _____

_____   _____   _____

TOTAL ANNUAL LIVING EXPENSES   _____   +   _____   =   _____

AMOUNT REMAINING FOR SAVINGS AND INVESTMENTS   _____

Projected Profit and Loss Statement
(Section 15 of the Business Plan)

Total Net Sales _____

Cost of Sales _____

GROSS PROFIT _____

Variable Expenses _____

Salaries _____

Taxes _____

Advertising _____

Delivery expense _____

Dues and subscriptions _____

Legal and other professional fees _____

Office supplies _____

Telephone _____

Utilities _____

Other _____

TOTAL VARIABLE EXPENSES _____

Fixed Expenses_____

Depreciation _____

Insurance _____

Rent or Mortgage _____

Taxes and Licenses _____

Loan payment (if applicable) _____

TOTAL FIXED EXPENSES _____

NET EXPENSES _____

NET PROFIT/LOSS (before taxes) _____

Cash Flow Projections for 19_____
(Section 15 of the Business Plan)

ANTICIPATED INCOME						MONTH						
	1	2	3	4	5	6	7	8	9	10	11	12
Cash sales												
Credit sales payments												
Other cash income												
TOTAL INCOME												

ANTICIPATED EXPENDITURES

	1	2	3	4	5	6	7	8	9	10	11	12
Cost of goods												
Wages												
Taxes												
Equipment expense												
Overhead												
Selling expense												
Advertising												
Transportation												
Delivery costs												
Loan repayment												
Other expenditures												
TOTAL EXPENDITURES												

Balance Sheet
(Section 15 of the Business Plan)

MONTH _____ YEAR _____

Current Assets

   Cash   _____

   Other investments   _____

   Accounts receivable   _____

   Inventory   _____

   Other assets   _____

TOTAL CURRENT ASSETS   _____

Intermediate and Fixed Assets

   Equipment and fixtures   _____

   Automobiles   _____

   Real estate   _____

   Other assets   _____

TOTAL INTERMEDIATE AND FIXED ASSETS   _____

TOTAL ASSETS   _____

Liabilities

   Accounts payable   _____

   Notes payable   _____

   Accrued expenses   _____

   Loans payable   _____

   Other liabilities   _____

TOTAL LIABILITIES   _____

Owner's equity   _____

TOTAL LIABILITIES AND OWNER'S EQUITY   _____

Raising Capital   Once you have a projected budget for the first year and an assessment of your assets and liabilities, you need to find sources of capital. Perhaps the simplest method of raising capital to start a home business is to save the money yourself. If you can manage to put aside money each payday, or if you already have a sizable bank account that could cover the capital needs of your business, you can eliminate or reduce considerable costs in interest later on. It's advisable to establish a separate business bank account as soon as possible. Doing so will enable you to keep your business money apart from your household and personal funds.

If necessary, consider the possibility of borrowing part of your start-up costs from family or friends. You may feel that this isn't a business-like approach to raising capital, but it certainly can be handled in a business-like manner. Just be sure you handle the loan as you would a loan with any financial institution. Have everything in writing—interest, terms of repayment, any penalties—to avoid the usual problems associated with borrowing from relatives. At least part of your financing may be secured in this way. Another possible source of funds is borrowing money against your life insurance policy if you've been paying premiums for a number of years.

Once you have explored the above sources of capital, you can approach a bank or savings and loan association. Such institutions generally require collateral, so you will be borrowing against your home, automobile, or other major possession. Some savings and loans have policies against loaning money for small business start-ups. Lending institutions in general may be wary of financing a home business, so it is important to impress them with the thoroughness of your business research and plans. Let bankers know how you plan to use the money and how you intend to pay it back. Impress upon the loan officer that you have raised some capital on your own, and let him or her know what your other sources of capital are. A banker might be more hesitant to risk money on your venture if it becomes apparent that you and your family and friends aren't willing to risk anything on it.

If your loan application is turned down, another source for funding is the Small Business Administration. As the SBA has limited funds, the majority of its financial assistance takes the form of guaranteeing loans which have previously been declined by a lending institution. In addition, the SBA supervises Small Business Investment Companies, a group of privately owned institutions that specialize in such loans under SBA regulations.

Finally, if your business is going to involve selling or

distributing a product, you might find that a major supplier of that product is willing to finance you, at least in part, by extending considerable credit to you initially. If you become really successful, he or she is going to receive a lot of business from you and, therefore, might be willing to help you get started or increase the size of your business.

Where Can I Get Capital?

The following is a list of possible sources of capital for beginning your business. As you investigate each possibility, indicate whether or not it is a workable source for you and indicate the amount you will be able to receive from that source. You will probably need to use several resources to obtain all of your start-up capital.

	No	Yes	Amount
Personal savings accounts	———	———	—————
Liquid investments such as stocks, bonds, and mutual funds	———	———	—————
Cash value of assets you could sell or use as collateral	———	———	—————
Cash value of life insurance	———	———	—————
Loan from relatives or friends	———	———	—————
Investment from a partner or other investor	———	———	—————
Home equity loan or other personal loan with collateral	———	———	—————
Commercial bank loan	———	———	—————
SBA micro-loan	———	———	—————
SBA loan guarantee	———	———	—————

Other Possible Sources:

	No	Yes	Amount
Chattel mortgages on equipment purchases	———	———	—————
Advance payment from contracts	———	———	—————
Trade credit in the form of delayed billing from suppliers	———	———	—————

Agencies that can help you secure financing

Small Business Investment Companies (SBICs) are licensed by the SBA. They make equity investments as well as loans.

The U.S. Small Business Administration will make direct loans as well as loan guarantees with other lending institutions.

State Business Development Agencies can provide guidance, programs, or services in the following areas:

- Business development

- Procurement assistance

- Financial assistance

- Opportunities for minorities and women

Tips for borrowing

- Develop a sound business plan, including figures on how you plan to use and repay borrowed capital. Well-thought-out plans inspire greater confidence in lenders.

- Never borrow more money than you can usefully employ in the business.

- Shop around with several lending institutions to get the best terms possible. Rates of interest do differ.

- It is generally cheaper to borrow on a short-term basis. Since cash flow may be a problem at the beginning, establish a line of credit and then only borrow as you need to.

- If you consider using a credit card loan for your business, be sure to compare the rate of interest with an ordinary business loan before you do so.

- Be careful about committing to a heavy repayment schedule in the early stage of your business.

- Don't overcommit yourself. It is better to start small and expand your business later. It may also be easier to get loans for expansion once you have had some proven success with your business in its early stages.

Setting Prices and Profit Margins

Once you have a realistic budget of your expenses, you should give serious consideration to the income side of your business. A common mistake made by new businesses is underpricing their services or products. Your prices must be high enough to cover all the overhead expenses you have just identified, plus make a profit. On the other hand, you cannot overprice your services, or clients will do business elsewhere.

Your market research should give you fairly detailed information about what the competition is charging for services or products equivalent to yours. You may find a considerable range of prices charged in certain lines of business. Typing services, for example, may vary widely in their charges for typing. One service may employ only top-notch typists using the latest word processing equipment, while another service might employ students typing in their spare time on whatever equipment they have or can borrow. In such cases as this, try to choose a price that accurately reflects your overhead and the quality of service you intend to provide.

Your tendency will be, no doubt, to price yourself lower than the competition, but this is often a mistake. Business people, in particular, are wary of services that are priced lower than usual. Their natural assumption is that such services must be offering inferior quality.

There are a number of formulas one can use to determine prices of either goods or services. Basically, you must consider the cost of producing the product or providing the service and add on the value of overhead costs. Next, estimate the volume of business you expect to do per month. Then determine your break-even price. Finally, add on a profit percentage that will cover your time and labor costs.

Income Forecasting Techniques

Income forecasting involves carefully estimating the profit you expect to make from your business based on probable volume of business, expenses that will need to be covered, and income of comparable businesses. Income forecasting can be important both in terms of deciding whether or not your business plans are feasible and in presenting plans to a bank in order to secure financing. First you must ascertain the minimum acceptable level of profit. Profit will be used to support personal living needs, to pay back borrowed funds, or to reinvest in the company.

To determine personal living requirements, consider the minimum amount you will need to withdraw from the business. If you plan to support yourself from a different source until your business gets off the ground, personal living expenses need not be taken from business profits.

For many home businesses, loan repayment of start-up capital is a major business expense. If it is necessary to borrow funds to begin the proposed business, these borrowed dollars will have to be repaid from the earnings of the business. To determine the level of profit necessary to repay a loan, you need to determine the dollar amount to be borrowed, the term of the loan, and the percent of interest likely to be charged. This type of calculation may be very important when presenting a business plan to a bank in order to secure a loan.

Income Forecasting Formula

1. The loan amount should equal the total amount of money needed to begin the business minus the amount supplied by you in the form of equity.

2. Calculation of the annual payment. Amount of loan, term of loan, total interest, and principle paid in one year.

3. Personal expenses + loan repayment = total profit to be generated in one year.

4. The next step is to determine the level of sales necessary to earn this profit level. To determine required annual sales volume:
   Required Profit = Minimum annual sales × Average percent profit

   Example: $23,600 = M × .11
   M = $214,500

5. Find the average profit for this type of business. You can determine average performance data from Annual Statement Studies, Dun and Bradstreet, the Bank of America, or local and national trade associations.

6. Once you have determined your minimum annual required sales, you can determine whether there is enough market potential to make this level of sales.

Before actually starting your business, reassess your plan. Focus on the following points:

- Can you raise the needed capital? Where and how will you do this?

- Can you obtain needed supplies?

- What are the risks you face?

- Last, and perhaps most important, do you have the ability to run the business, and are you willing to put in the time and effort needed?

Your business plan should be detailed and well thought out before you actually start running your business. In this way you can anticipate many likely problems and perhaps find ways to circumvent them.

Once you have considered the areas covered in this chapter and have carefully conceived and laid out your plans, you are ready to start your business. It's very important not to shortchange the phase of planning and setting up your business. Costly errors and problems can be avoided if you carefully research and learn about every aspect of your business before you jump into it with both feet. It should be apparent that a tremendous amount of planning, devotion, and hard work go into creating and maintaining a successful home-based business. But the rewards of running your own business can make it well worth your efforts.

Operating Your Business

Once you have carefully laid out your business plan and secured financing, you are ready to start your home-based enterprise. Operating a home-based business presents many of the same challenges and problems as other types of businesses; however, some considerations and ways of doing things are unique to cottage industries.

Working Environment

At first glance it seems too obvious to even discuss the working environment of a home-based business. Everyone knows what the home environment is like; to describe this environment seems redundant and even silly. At second glance, however, we begin to realize that we are less familiar with the concept of a home business setting than with almost any other type of work environment. In what ways does the home working environment differ from that of the traditional work site?

Multiple functions   The most fundamental difference is that the sole function of an office is to house a business, but a home with a business being run from it serves multiple functions. Not only does a home under these circumstances house a business, but it also provides shelter for a family.

Consequently, a home business may have to contend with a great deal of activity on the premises that is not business related. Distractions—such as personal phone calls, demands of family members, and household responsibilities—will require that the home business person develop discipline and coping strategies to either deal with, or ignore, these extraneous activities. Therefore, it is important that the home business have a permanent location in the home, preferably one that will not be disturbed by other family members.

If your home business situation is such that you live alone or other family members are absent from the home during the day, opposite circumstances may be true. Your home office may have very few distractions. This may enable you to be more productive than in a traditional office. In fact, the greater part of your working day may be spent alone, to the point that isolation may become a problem if you don't work to circumvent it. Negative aspects of isolation are discussed at greater length in chapter 2.

Ways to separate work from home life

- Plan a fifteen minute break from work before your evening begins.

- Run errands after work to provide distance from your work day.

- Keep regular office hours. Label working outside those hours as overtime.

- Don't use your office for purposes other than work.

- As much as possible, keep the work area physically separated from your other living space, particularly when your work day is done.

- Don't go back into your office after leaving it for the day.

- Have a separate business phone and don't answer it after business hours. If letting it ring annoys you, you can invest in an answering machine or service.

- Meet with colleagues in your field during lunch or after hours. Such networking reinforces the idea of leaving an office.

Informal atmosphere

A second aspect unique to the home work environment is that it can be much more reflective of the individual working there. As a worksteader, you can make the work area as much or as little like a traditional job setting as desired, within the constraints of the demands of your tasks and your budget. You can also feel free to incorporate into your work environment whatever is comfortable or attractive to you. Consequently, many home work spaces tend to be more informal than traditional offices.

More than in perhaps any other type of employment, home businesses allow the individual control over the work environment. This fact is of great importance to workers with special needs, physical or otherwise, since these needs may be more easily accommodated in the home setting.

Notwithstanding the desire to individualize the environment, most home businesses having clientele that regularly enter their homes strive to make the home office as businesslike in appearance as possible. Since the customers' impressions are important to the success of your business, your office should reflect the fact that you take your business seriously. While this doesn't mean that you need to remove all the comforts of home from your working area, too many homey touches and distracting elements may undermine your image of professionalism.

Selecting Your Home Office Space

List your business space requirements.

1. Minimum space needs (approximate dimensions). _____

   _____

2. Separate entrance required? _____

3. Entrance open to or separate from the rest of the house? _____

4. Expenses necessary to fix up or make the area suitable for business needs. _____

   _____

5. Extra furniture and supplies needed. _____

   _____

   _____

   _____

6. Other considerations: _____

   _____

   _____

   _____

List possible alternative sites in your home.

Alternative #1							
Alternative #2							
Alternative #3							
Alternative #4							
Space Requirements	**#1**	**#2**	**#3**	**#4**	**#5**	**#6**	**Total**

Rank each alternative.

Rank each alternative from one to four for each of your space requirements. Then total the points for each site alternative. The site with the most points will be the best choice for the location of a business in your home.

Adaptation to business needs

Home business working environments understandably differ in accord with the type of business being run. Depending on the needs of an individual enterprise, a home office can be as simple as a folding table and chair in the corner of a bedroom or as elaborate as a remodeled office complete with filing cabinets, office equipment, impressive office furniture, and microcomputer.

Some businesses require special equipment and supplies, such as woodworking tools if you custom build cabinets, or a personal computer and peripheral equipment if you run a word processing business.

Laying Out Your Business Space

ITEM NEEDED	HAVE	NEED TO PURCHASE
Desk		
File cabinet		
Storage Shelves		
Desk Chair		
Telephone		
Typewriter		
Occasional Chairs		
Table		
Special Equipment		
Other Needs		

In the space below you can sketch the layout of your business space. Use pencil so you can make any necessary changes.

Numerous types of home businesses are often best suited to being carried on either outdoors or in some type of outbuilding such as a garage, barn, or studio. Potters, painters, furniture refinishers, antique restorers, pet groomers, and kennel operators are just a few examples of such enterprises. Space, environmental, or safety considerations may make it unwise or undesirable to operate certain businesses from the same area in which you eat and sleep.

Some home businesses are not typically thought of as home enterprises because their basic operations are carried out exclusively on premises away from the home. These enterprises include house painting, grading and trucking services, plumbing and electrical contracting, and a host of other sales and service functions. Even for businesses of this type, however, a home office of some kind is necessary, although it need not be as elaborate as an office that houses all aspects of a business.

Since these businesses still have bookkeeping, billing, and other paperwork to deal with, some office furniture and equipment will be needed. Perhaps a desk and a filing cabinet may be all that are necessary. Many of these businesses, on the other hand, also utilize specialized equipment and have special storage needs. In such cases the home office would have to allow for the storage of such equipment when not in use, as well as the storage of parts and materials commonly used in the practice or production of that particular trade.

Because these businesses bring the entrepreneur into frequent contact with the public outside the home, day-to-day routine will be much more varied in terms of work location, customers seen, and even in working conditions encountered.

New home designs

As the trend toward home businesses is being taken more seriously by society, some architects are beginning to include accommodations for home businesses in their home designs. Predictions of growth in telecommuting have had especially significant impact in this respect. Many architects, for instance, are projecting the need for home designs which incorporate computer work stations in living areas.

If you are thinking of building a new house or expanding your present home, consider contacting an architect attuned to this movement. Futurist Alvin Toffler predicts that this country will move toward "demassification" of industry, education, and communication. As a result, suburban areas could become predominantly centers of work and social activity, while urban centers might decline in importance. Toffler urges the home building industry to anticipate the changing economic and social conditions in order to prepare for different housing needs of the expanding group of home workers, many of whom fit his concept of "third wave" electronic cottage industries.

Daily Business Operation

For whatever type of business the home entrepreneur elects to run, the day-to-day operation of that business presents several issues which deserve attention. Your daily business routine will greatly affect your life-style and the satisfaction that your work gives you.

Scheduling business hours

One of the advantages of a home business is that you can decide what your hours will be. Remember, though, that in order for your hours to be most beneficial for your business, they must meet your customers' needs as well as your own. Therefore, set your business hours with your customers' convenience in mind. Usually, traditional business hours are the easiest for everyone involved, but the type of business you run may dictate that evening, early morning, or weekend hours are necessary. It is important that your hours be consistent so that your clients can rely on them. If you choose not to be open for business every day or to close early certain days, make your "off" times part of a permanent schedule.

It's also good business sense to make use of an answering machine or service so that customers can leave messages when you are not working or are out of the office. Return their calls promptly, for if you don't, you risk losing their business.

Serving your customers

Regardless of the type of business you operate, the function of your business is to fulfill your customers' needs. Good service, quality products and services, and fair prices are essential to keep your customers coming back. Let your customers know that you appreciate their patronage by treating them with courtesy, friendliness, and a genuine interest in serving their needs to the best of your ability. Presenting a professional image through your appearance and business practices will also make a favorable impression on your clients.

Capitalize on the personal nature of your home business. Stress your friendly, personalized service because it is a major advantage you have over large, impersonal stores and firms. You can do this, in part, by offering little extras such as personal consultations on gift or wardrobe selections, gift wrapping, accepting rush orders, and making sure that customer complaints are resolved to the clients' satisfaction. Your goal should be to build goodwill between you and your customers and to strive for customer satisfaction so that your clients will keep coming back and also recommend your business to others.

Keeping up with business demands

Working in a home business, you may find that there just aren't enough hours in a day. Since most home entrepreneurs work alone, the majority of business responsibilities fall on just one person. Many home business owners find that they must work considerably more than forty hours a week to keep up with the amount of work necessary to earn a living.

Catching up with business demands once you have fallen behind can be a monumental task under these conditions. Therefore, keeping up with your work is essential. This also holds true for record keeping and other paperwork, areas which are easy to neglect when you are hurrying to meet product deadlines or finish a particular job. The following tips may help you keep up with business demands:

Be efficient. First, streamline your business as much as possible. This means eliminating unnecessary tasks and simplifying necessary work. Use an efficient record-keeping system which allows you to keep your entries to a minimum. Stop writing personal responses to every letter of inquiry; instead, send a brochure or form letter for routine matters.

Plan your time. Second, make maximum use of your time. Avoid distractions whenever possible. Find a pattern which allows you to produce the most work in a given period. For example, assembly-line styled production may make far more productive use of your time than constructing one complete product at a time. Also, plan your day in advance so you won't have to waste time making unnecessary trips or waiting for customers or suppliers.

Get help. Third, delegate some of the responsibilities that are not essential for you to do personally. Any task that you pay someone else to do frees your time for work you must see to yourself. Hiring someone at relatively low wages to do time-consuming tasks such as stuffing envelopes, packaging your products, or making deliveries is often well worth the price. You need not hire someone full-time or on a permanent basis if that doesn't fit your needs. Many students and other people are eager to earn a little extra money and aren't concerned with permanent, full-time employment.

Ideas regarding the selection of employees are covered in more detail in chapter 7. While that chapter deals with product-oriented businesses, many of the ideas in reference to hiring help would also apply to service businesses.

In summary, to make sure that you keep up with your business demands:

- Plan your time carefully to assure yourself of a productive work day.

- Organize your business tasks well to save yourself time and effort.

- Get extra help if you need it.

Making the most of your business hours often means you can do a larger volume of business and add to your profits. And that's why you're in business.

Marketing

For many people, marketing poses a number of problems and promotes uncertainty and confusion. We are all aware that good marketing of a product or service is often critical to the success of a business, but we're not sure what type of marketing is best. We want the competitive edge, but we're not sure how to obtain it.

Marketing is the key to success for most small businesses. As a home business owner, you will want to consider new and unique ways of reaching customers, in addition to the more common or familiar marketing strategies.

The least costly way for you as a business owner to reach customers is to have them come to your home to buy and pick up your product or service. But there are a variety of other ways to market one's product or service if your home is too hard to find, if many of your customers don't drive, or if it is inconvenient for whatever reason to have customers coming to your home.

Consider the following ideas to market your goods or service:

- Make sales on the telephone and have customers pick up the product.

- Sell on the telephone and deliver the product.

- Sell door-to-door (most locales require a street trades' permit for this.)

- Sell at parties in customers' homes.

- Use direct mail sales and deliver your materials to the customer.

- Use direct mail sales and ship the product.

- Sell from a van, truck, or trailer.

- Sell at farmers' markets, county fairs, or church bazaars.

- Contact shopping centers that have antique, art, and hobby theme shows at which you can sell your product.

- Investigate leasing department space in a retail store.

- Franchise your business and teach others how to start their own branches.

- Sell wholesale to retail stores.

- Supply fund-raising ideas to groups using your products.

Marketing techniques will demand careful planning, aggressive approaches, and creative thinking. In addition to the ideas listed, you may conceive of many new ways of your own to reach customers.

Marketing Ideas

What marketing tool(s) can you implement within your budget? _____

_____

_____

How can you test your marketing ideas? _____

_____

_____

How can you measure the results of a market test or campaign? _____

_____

_____

Which new marketing tool can you implement right now? _____

_____

_____

Choose Your Methods of Communication:

Advertising.   Which types are appropriate for your business? _____

_____

_____

Co-op Advertising.   How can you tap this resource? _____

_____

_____

Word of Mouth.   How can you leverage this highly credible communications tool? _____

_____

_____

Telephone Directories.   How can you make them more effective? Under how many different headings could you list your business?

_____

_____

_____

_____

Direct Mail.   Can you target a specific customer/develop a comprehensive list/provide an incentive to visit your store?

_____

_____

Collateral.   Are you making use of all the point-of-purchase and merchandising opportunities available to you? _____

_____

_____

Promotion.   Would contests, seminars, or demonstrations work for you? _____

_____

_____

Publicity.   Is your company's name in the media? What could you do to get it there? _____

_____

_____

As a new business person, you may be tempted to try to be all things to all people in order to gain more business. To get the most from your marketing attempts, you need to target your promotion sales and efforts. Your goal is to reach the largest number of potential customers at the lowest possible price. Marketing is not working effectively when you are either reaching the wrong people or are spending too much to reach the right people.

Two key concepts involved in marketing are segmentation and positioning. *Segmentation* involves selecting a portion of the total market that you feel you are best suited to serve. Perhaps your service has a particular twist which makes it most suitable for small business customers. If so, target your marketing to reach that segment of the market population.

Positioning means that for each segment of the market you serve, you need to develop a marketing plan that will appeal to people in that particular segment. Each market segment will have slightly different needs, tastes, and wants. You will thus need to answer the following questions for each market segment you hope to serve:

- Product or Service—What is it and what can it do for your prospect?

- How will you get the product or service to the customer?

- Price—How much can you charge? Will your volume of sales make the business successful at that price?

- Promotion—What can you say or do to attract customers to your proposition and what will the cost of such promotion be?

Advertising and Publicity

Few areas of a business present as great a challenge as promotion and advertising. Large amounts of money are spent each year on business promotion. All too often, much of that money is wasted on ineffective and ill-considered advertising. If your budget for promotion is limited, it is all the more important that every dollar count.

The most important advertising effort is a listing in the yellow pages of your local phone directory. Other essential promotional items are business stationery and business cards. Using printed stationery immediately sets the tone that you are a serious business person. A well-designed letterhead can also serve as the basis for press releases or basic informational literature.

While it's not usually wise to skimp on promoting your business, try to follow up on the various types of advertising you select to determine which means are doing the most cost-effective job of bringing your customers to you.

Advertising strategies

Logo. Develop an eye-catching distinctive symbol for your business that will make people notice and remember you. Use this logo on your business cards, stationery, product labels, bills, and signs and in advertising to help you achieve recognition in the marketplace.

Signs. If your zoning regulations permit it, use a professional looking sign to advertise your business. Not only will it help people to locate your business, but it helps to further name recognition and is a low cost form of advertising.

Word of mouth. The best way to achieve word-of-mouth advertising is by giving customers good products and services for their money. You can encourage customers to spread the word by giving out extra business cards, asking customers if you can use them as a reference, and by offering special deals for customers who bring in friends, such as two-for-one specials. You can also ask customers for recommendations of friends who could use your services or products.

Flyers. Most businesses will require several items of basic literature that describe your services, products, and prices. For many purposes, simply typing up a flyer on your business letterhead and then having it duplicated by photo offset printing will be adequate. This type of flyer can be distributed in your neighborhood and slipped under windshield wipers at the shopping center parking lot.

You might also try targeting distribution to potential clients. For example, if your business is one that small business persons might use, you could hand deliver your flyer to merchants along the adjacent streets. Such flyers frequently result in more business than a newspaper ad which costs many times more.

If you intend to send out mailings, you might want to invest a little more money and have a brochure or flyer typeset. Find a typographer who will give you both fast service and a good price. You will find that quotes will vary widely from firm to firm. If you pay for the piece being typeset, request the master when you pick up your flyers. Many typographers simply throw them away, but you can reuse masters a number of times.

Direct mailings. This is the most personalized and targeted of all media. Its flexibility allows for telling a complete story by letter or brochure or special promotions with a post card. This is a highly selective media. When you have a basic literature piece, consider sending out a mailing. While more expensive than hand-delivered flyers, it is still much cheaper than most display or classified newspaper advertisements.

There are a number of sources for mailing lists, including list rental firms. To start, you could make a mailing list of friends and acquaintances who might be interested. Using the telephone directory's yellow pages, you might also compile lists of business people who could be potential customers. If you think certain neighborhoods might be especially suitable, you can even get voter registration lists. They are public documents, and you are entitled to copies of them.

If possible, keep a copy of any mailing list you use. If you get a good response, you may want to circulate the same list six months or a year later. In time, you will build up a valuable list of clients that you can rent to others. Some firms actually make as much money from renting their lists as they do from providing the original sales or services.

A word of caution is in order regarding either buying or selling mailing lists. Some firms sell or rent mailing labels or lists for limited or one-time use. To assure that this is not violated, they seed the lists, often paying a number of people to use a coded version of their names and addresses and to forward any mailings they receive to the mailing list firm.

When putting out a mailing, always include newspaper editors and columnists. By doing so, you may receive a free mention in the press or a referral. Also, send one of the mailing pieces to yourself. In this way you can determine when your mailing actually has been received by those on the mailing list.

It is also a good practice to experiment with different types of mailing pieces to appeal to different tastes. Try a rather formal, informative, and tasteful brochure to supply basic information in addition to an upbeat, eye-catching piece that is convenient for the client to put away for future reference.

Promotional items. There are a number of useful promotional items that you can order from advertising specialty firms. All types of things can be imprinted with your business name, phone number, and address. Items which are especially popular with customers include pens, pencils, matchbooks, balloons, pocket engagement calendars, and refrigerator magnets—all imprinted with your business name and phone number. When selecting such promotional items, try to pick something that is of good quality, will be constantly in front of the customer, and used frequently.

Advertisements. One of the most unpredictable facets of any business is advertising. Sometimes very expensive ads will be totally ineffective, whereas a two-line classified ad can often produce remarkable results. Many ad-takers working for newspapers are paid by the line; consequently, they will try to get you to take a larger ad than you may need. In most ads, all you basically need is your business name, the nature of your business (if that's not readily apparent from your business name), and your phone number or address if your business is primarily mail order.

Even if you want to include more information in your print ads, keep them short and to the point. Write ads so that they compel the reader to take action. Include in your ads words that have been shown to get results. Here are a few:

new	easy
discovery	safe
free	save
money	you
proven	love
money-back	health
guarantee	

Most advertising managers advise that frequency of advertising is more persuasive than ad size, so choose smaller ads which appear more often. Many people will hesitate to contact a business they have just learned about; but if they see the name week after week, they assume that it is established and reliable.

If you run ads concurrently in more than one place, be sure to code your ads so you know which ad drew a response. Code telephone number ads by stating "Ask for Mary" in one ad and "Ask for Helen" in another. An ad featuring an address can be keyed by adding initials after the box number or street address, such as P.O. Box 6421–D, or 2143–D South Myrtle Drive. In this way you'll know which ads are the most effective.

Co-op advertising. Your suppliers may agree to pay half the cost of advertising that mentions their products. This is called co-op advertising. If you are able to use this approach, check with your supplier; he or she may even be able to supply you with prepared ad copy, thus saving you even more time and money.

Major advertising media

Under some circumstances you may want to consider advertising through some form of mass media. While mass media ads are generally quite expensive, they do provide a great deal of exposure for your business and can be quite effective. For most home businesses you will want to wait until you're having some success with your business before investing a lot of money in mass advertising. Even then, carefully weigh your decision in terms of cost versus ad effectiveness.

Newspapers. Newspaper ads are best used for advertising more detailed information about your products or service and for promoting special events or sales. It is better to use small ads that appear on a consistent basis so that customers develop a sense of trust in your business.

Local television. The major advantage of television is that it has a large audience with high visibility. Television provides instant exposure of pictures and ideas and is also good for name awareness and product demonstration. Among television's drawbacks are its comparatively high cost and potentially reaching the wrong market.

Local radio. Radio is a flexible medium that allows targeting customer groups via distinctive programming. This type of advertising is useful for building awareness and advertising special promotions. This is a selective media, purchased according to demographic profiles.

Trade publications. This print media is mostly used for targeting business-to-business customers. As print media, trade publications allow for more information about a product or service. This type of advertising has the advantage of being market segmented; you have a better chance of targeting and reaching the market segment you desire. Specialty magazines and publications also target your market in much the same way, such as advertising a computer accessory in a computer magazine.

Outdoor signs. This is a highly visible media and gives very broad awareness. Its best use is for name identification and image. Outdoor signs may not be selective enough if your market segment is a limited one.

Yellow pages. The yellow pages may prove to be the best buy for your advertising dollars. A mass medium by content and distribution, it also has the ability to target market segments. No other media is as effective in market penetration. Advertisers are accessible to all potential customers 24 hours a day, 365 days a year.

Remember, these are mass media and, with the exception of a yellow pages ad, may not be cost effective for your business. Many home businesses use some of these advertising media with excellent results.

Selecting Advertising Media

The following questions can help you decide which advertising media will be best for your business.

Who uses your product or service? _____

_____

_____

How does the consumer benefit from your product or service? _____

_____

_____

Where and when do you want to reach your prospective customers? _____

_____

_____

How many potential customers do you need to reach? How often do you want to reach them? _____

_____

_____

How much can you afford to spend? _____

_____

_____

Publicity   Briefly stated, mention in the media that you pay for is *advertising*; any mention you don't pay for is *publicity*. Consequently, one can look at publicity as free advertising. If your advertising budget is small, as it is for most home businesses, try first for as much publicity as you can get.

If you have a unique aspect to your business, are doing something for the public, can offer yourself as a guest speaker on radio or television, or can write an article for the newspaper, you can get what amounts to free advertising. And since any of this appears to be a news story, it lends credibility that an ad may not have. In effect, you get the endorsement of the media.

Getting free mention in the press isn't always easy. There are, however, several things you can do in order to increase your chances of getting media coverage for your business. If your business is somewhat unusual, inform the media in your area about your business to see if they'd like to do a story about it. Many newspapers and television news shows like to run human interest stories, and unusual home businesses are often perfect for this.

Whenever something noteworthy occurs in your business, such as your grand opening, an unusual promotion, or some special offering such as free classes about some aspect of your business, write a press release describing the event and send copies to all the media contacts in your area. Hopefully, one or more will run it as a story. When writing a press release, make sure that it is concise and well written. This is important because newspapers often print a press release "as is." If your press release is poorly written, the newspaper may decide not to use it at all. Newspapers sometimes only use the first paragraph or two of a press release, so make sure that all the vital information is contained in these paragraphs.

If you win an award in conjunction with your business or have some distinction bestowed upon you or your product, inform the press. They may make a brief mention of it in their paper.

As you can see, the most important element in getting free publicity is to contact the media yourself. By doing so, you make the media aware of your business and greatly increase your chances of gaining publicity. Any mention you receive in the media will enhance public recognition of your business and bring more customers to your door.

As stories and articles mentioning your business appear, begin a scrapbook to preserve a record. Your chances of getting further mention in the media are greatly enhanced if you can show a reporter what has already been printed about you in the press.

Accounting and Bookkeeping Needs

In looking at the financial considerations for starting a home business, it should become apparent that accurate financial records and written budget plans are a must. If accounting and bookkeeping are a mystery to you, don't hesitate to hire an accountant or bookkeeper to keep your accounts. As experienced professionals, accountants can also offer advice on taxes and other financial matters that can give your business a better chance of being successful.

If you want to do your own bookkeeping, there are courses in bookkeeping available through vocational and technical schools as well as numerous books on the subject. If you have a home computer, there are many software packages for keeping accounts. Whether you use a computer for bookkeeping or do it manually, make sure the bookkeeping system you select is easy for you to use and understand.

For most home businesses, the two-journal system is probably the easiest to implement and to understand. In your Cash Receipts Journal, you record all money coming into your business. For each entry, be sure to include the date, the source, and what the money was for. In your Cash Disbursements Journal, record all the money that goes out from your business. For each entry, include what the expense was, the date, and to whom the payment was made. Sample journal pages are included here to give an idea of how you could set up your books.

Cash Receipts Journal

Date	Source	Total Receipts	Merchandise Sales	Service Sales	Taxes	Miscellaneous

Cash Disbursements Journal

Date	Check	Payee	Description	Total Paid	Inventory	Supplies

Accounting methods

Simply put, there are two basic methods of accounting, the cash method and the accrual method. When using the *cash method* you report all income in the year you receive it. You deduct business expenses in the year you pay them.

If you use the *accrual method* of accounting, you report income in the year you earn it regardless of when you actually receive it. You also deduct expenses in the tax year you incur them, regardless of when you pay them. If your business has an inventory, you must generally use the accrual method for purchases and sales.

Keep good records

Since every business deals with a constant flow of business expenses, sales, and inventory purchases, good record keeping is essential. As you progress in your business, you will find that good records accomplish the following:

1. Prevent omission of deductible expenses.

2. Establish earnings for self-employment tax purposes.

3. Explain items on income tax returns. You must be able to support items on your return with sales slips, invoices, receipts, bank deposit slips, cancelled checks, and other documents.

Regardless of the accounting method you use, be sure to identify the source of each receipt. Unless you have records showing the source of your receipts, you may not be able to prove that some are nonbusiness or nontaxable.

Taxes   One of the greatest benefits of running a home business today, aside from rent-free business space, is the tax advantages available to the home business person. For this reason, the Internal Revenue Service is very exacting in its
requirements for home businesses. Records of the business
must be meticulously kept. It's important to be aware that
while losses from a side business may be deducted from the
earnings of a primary job, the IRS definition of a business
stipulates that the business must show a profit two consec-
utive years in any five-year period.

What tax advantages are associated with a home business? The answer to this question is partially dependent on
what type of legal structure you have chosen for your
business.

In order to qualify for home business tax deductions,
you must meet certain tests or requirements outlined by
the IRS. Basically, the part of your home for which you are
claiming deductions must be used both exclusively and
regularly as one or more of the following:

- The principal place of business for any trade or
  business in which you engage

  or
- A place to meet or deal with your patients, clients, or
  customers in the normal course of your trade or
  business

  or
- A structure that is not attached to your house or
  residence and that is used in connection with your
  trade or business

If you use your home for work as an employee, the use
of your home must be for the convenience of your employer
as well as meet one of the above requirements. This has
significance for home workers engaged in telecommuting,
which is discussed in chapter 8. You may also deduct expenses that relate to the use of part of your home for storage of inventory.

In any given year, deductions that are indirectly related
to your business cannot exceed the gross earnings of the
business use of your home. Indirect expenses are those expenses you have for upkeep and running of the entire
home. Such expenses include real estate taxes, mortgage
interest, rent, utilities and services, insurance, repairs,
and depreciation. The business portions of these expenses
are deductible. Direct expenses that benefit only the business part of your home, which might include painting and
repairs to your work area, are fully deductible.

This brief summary is quite simplistic. The IRS publishes special guidelines to assist the home business person in figuring his or her tax deductions. Also available from the IRS are tax packages for the self-employed and small businesses. Both of these can also be very helpful to the home entrepreneur. If you need an accountant to help you with your taxes, be sure to use one. In the long run, you can't afford costly mistakes.

Of course, having a home business also means you have to pay taxes. Any business venture is subject to income tax if it makes a profit. If your business is unincorporated, profits are subject to self-employment tax, which is Social Security. Generally, self-employment and income taxes on business profits must be paid in quarterly installments on an estimated tax voucher (form 1040ES). This procedure is explained in detail in the IRS publication 533, *Self-Employment Tax.*

State taxes are another important matter, since most states also have their own state income taxes. These vary greatly in their structure, so it is difficult to offer any generalized advice regarding them. Consult your state tax office to gain information on these taxes and check with an accountant if you need help.

Home Business Insurance Needs

Nearly every type of business, whether in-home or not, requires insurance protection of one form or another. Yet many people starting home businesses fail to consider their insurance needs. A carefully planned insurance program is vital to the protection of your business and personal assets from unforeseen losses and significant financial burdens.

There are several types of insurance coverage that the home business owner should consider. Your particular business may not require all of these forms of insurance, but you will probably need at least a few of the following types of coverage:

- Liability—product liability and workmen's compensation

- Burglary, theft, and robbery

- Fire

- Business life

- Credit

- Fidelity bonds and security bonds

Since your business will be located in your home, your homeowner's policy may cover such risks as fire and theft. Check with your insurance agent to determine the extent of coverage which your homeowner's policy affords you. Homeowner's insurance does not necessarily cover business activities. If your insurance coverage is not adequate for the business portion of your home, you may be able to purchase a rider that will extend your insurance to cover the additional value of your business materials. If a rider is not possible, you may have to take out a separate policy to cover your business against fire and theft.

For other types of insurance coverage, you can get whatever information you need from an insurance agent or broker. When organizing your business insurance program, take the following steps:

- Define the different perils your business may face and rank them according to which present the greatest loss risk.

- Study your insurance costs, including any methods you can take to reduce coverage costs.

- Cover your largest risk first.

- Shop around for the best, most cost-effective coverage, as all insurance coverage is not the same.

- Prepare an insurance plan that is compatible with your operation and goals.

- Avoid duplicate coverage.

- Get professional advice from a qualified insurance agent, broker, or consultant, who can explain options and recommend the best and least costly coverage.

- Periodically review your insurance program, as your coverage needs may change.

Since insurance coverage is an important and complex matter, you are well advised to work closely with your insurance broker or agent so that you purchase insurance which best suits your needs. To protect yourself, any change in your business operation that might affect insurance needs should be discussed promptly with your insurance agent.

Hiring Professionals   Unless you are unusually knowledgeable, you are going to need professional help in at least one or two areas of your home business. Think about whether or not you need the help or advice of an attorney, accountant, banker, public relations or advertising expert, graphics specialist, writer, or any other professional whose expertise meets your needs.

Home business novices often make the mistake of trying to do everything themselves, whether they are good at it or not. Don't succumb to this pitfall. Get the help you need from competent, reliable professionals, and you won't regret it.

When looking for professional services, try to avoid bargain hunting. A good accountant who charges higher fees, for instance, may actually save you more money than paying for the difference in fees. In any event, ask professionals in advance what their services will cost. They expect you to seek this information, and you need it in planning your business budget.

When looking for professional help, ask other business people for recommendations. When you talk to a person whom you are considering hiring, don't be hesitant to ask for samples of work, referrals, or whatever else might be necessary to determine the quality of that person's services.

Service Businesses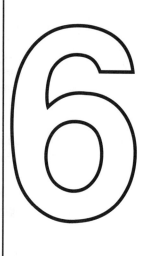

The most rapidly expanding area of at-home business involves service businesses. Simply defined, a *service business* is one that provides a service for a fee, as opposed to producing a product. The service may be performed for an individual or for another business. Generally, service businesses perform jobs for people which they either cannot or prefer not do for themselves.

The United States economy has been undergoing dynamic change as it moves from domination by manufacturing businesses to service-related enterprises. Since 1982, service and information-related businesses have continued to represent the fastest growing industrial sector of our economy. Studies from the government report *State of Small Business in 1986* show that since 1981, fourteen and a half million jobs have been created, and nearly all of these jobs have come from small business starts and expansions.

More than one half of the newly created jobs were developed from the service sector that was dominated by small business owners. Of the more than 17.3 million small businesses reporting to the Internal Revenue Service, 13 million were proprietorships and 1.4 million were partnerships. These were primarily self-employed individuals who found their career opportunities in the growing field of small business services.

Personal and Corporate Services

Service businesses focusing on personal services, or work performed for an individual, include an almost endless list of businesses including, but in no way limited to, hairdressing, color analysis, wardrobe consulting, household organization, dog grooming, lawn maintenance, snow removal, tax consulting, catering, cleaning and party services, house painting, and interior decorating.

Personal services come in a wide variety of sizes and forms. Think about an individual performing a skilled service for another for a fee, in some cases modest, in others handsome. A seamstress and a theatrical agent provide examples of service businesses on a one-to-one basis. At the other end of the size spectrum, imagine operating a business employing several or many people to perform services for numerous clients. A home care service and a lawn care company might serve as examples of larger, more complex service businesses.

Among other personal services that can be operated from the home, consider the following: insurance agents; tax consultants; real estate agents; day-care centers; home guardians; caretakers for the elderly; counselors; music, art, and dance instructors; nursing services; employment agencies; tutors and teachers of any special skills; and maintenance and repair services of all kinds. One thing all these personal services have in common—they serve individuals and, in one way or another, help make life easier, safer, or more pleasurable.

Services performed for businesses or corporations constitute an important source of work, and when one has established a good reputation, it is surprising how many businesses will hire outside services for a variety of jobs. Services provided to businesses include typing or word processing, graphic arts, accounting, clipping services, telephone answering, and housekeeping and maintenance duties.

Advantages of Service Businesses

Most service businesses share some characteristics that make them particularly well suited to operation from home.

No inventory. Perhaps the most obvious advantage is that, since one is selling a service rather than a product, the person doesn't have to be concerned with keeping an inventory of products on hand. Consequently, for most service businesses, very little actual office or work space is required.

Low start-up costs. A second advantage is that many service businesses need only limited equipment and supplies in order to provide the services; therefore start-up costs can be kept low. In fact, there are many service businesses that require no special equipment other than what you probably already own.

Low profile. Depending on whether you perform the service in your home or at some other location, service businesses may be less disruptive or noticeable to your neighbors and your own family than a product-oriented business. Consider an office-cleaning business. Since the service is performed outside your home and most likely outside your neighborhood, clients need not come to your residence. This means that your family life will not be disturbed, nor will you have to be concerned with parking for your customers or disturbing your neighbors. In fact, with a service such as this, your home business will be nearly invisible in the neighborhood.

Even if you perform the service in your home—word processing, for example—service businesses may be less intrusive than product-oriented businesses. Pick up and delivery can be made a part of your service, or you can limit pick-up and delivery hours to coincide with times that are convenient for your particular situation.

Small-scale operation. Service businesses also make good cottage industries because they are well suited to a small-scale operation. For the home business with one or two employees, services tend to be more lucrative because there are no raw goods to pay for, and it is not generally necessary to tie up funds in an extensive inventory. A service business can be run by one person and either intentionally kept small or, as demand arises, expanded by hiring other employees. Check the ideas in chapter 7 if you consider hiring helpers.

Emphasis on skill and time. It's easier to be competitive in a service line of business than in most product businesses because a service requires time and skill, both factors under control of the home entrepreneur. A product business item, on the other hand, may be more cheaply made in a production line or with mass purchase of raw materials.

Based on these obvious advantages, it's clear that anyone desiring to start a home enterprise should seriously consider a service business. Remember to study potential markets and analyze your own skills. With the right combination, you may have the makings of a very profitable home business.

Considering a Service Business

- What special skills or talents do you possess that might be the basis of a home business? _____

_____

_____

- Is there a demand for any of these services in your area? _____

_____

_____

- Are any special materials or equipment required for this business? How much would they cost?

_____

_____

- What other overhead costs do you foresee? _____

_____

_____

- Can you set your prices competitively and still make a fair wage? _____

_____

_____

Pricing and Permits

When setting prices for a service business, don't overlook the cost of all of the materials used. Depending on the business, it may be important also to determine ahead of time who will provide particular supplies. If you decide to run a wallpaper hanging service, for example, you will probably provide drop cloths, ladders, rollers, paste, and other equipment and materials—all necessary for performing the job. The customer may expect to pay only for the wallpaper selected. If you expect the customer to provide protection such as drop cloths for furniture, for example, your customers should be advised of this beforehand, and your price should be somewhat lower than if you had provided drop cloths. In any case, your prices should reflect the quality and extent of service you are providing.

In a service business, you should bill all direct costs separately. Examples of direct costs include a photographer's film, a management consultant's trip to the plant, and a publicist's cab fare and long-distance phone calls. If you bill these items separately, you can distinguish between the cost of your professional services and direct business expenses which you pass on to your customer. This simplifies bookkeeping and makes it possible for you to keep your fee the same, even if the postal rate or the price of transportation goes up. Increases in these areas are often more readily accepted by customers than an increase in wages.

Despite not having the costs of producing a product, a service business will still have overhead: phone calls that can't be billed to clients, salaries, taxes, promotional materials, mailings to new clients, and expenses associated with the daily operation of your business, such as maintaining your work area and materials. To price a job, you can charge either an hourly rate, calculated to cover your overhead plus a decent income for yourself, or charge a flat rate per job. It seems almost too obvious to mention, but many people ignore the fact that you must set your prices high enough to make your work profitable while at the same time low enough to attract customers in the competitive marketplace.

Permits and licenses

Most food services, such as catering, require special consideration. You must realize that most states have stringent health laws which may preclude certain types of food preparation from being done in the home. Make sure you can meet these regulations before embarking on any food-related service.

Another caution is necessary. Certain service businesses require state license for their practice. Hairdressing and care for the young, old, or infirm when involving certain numbers of clients are just two examples of services that require licensing in many states. You may also need to ascertain whether or not your city requires special training or license for performing certain services.

Franchising Opportunities

A particular type of service business that you might consider is a franchise business. *Franchising* is a form of business where the owner, or *franchisor,* gives license to distribute products, services, or methods of business at the retail level to affiliated dealers, or *franchisees.* In many cases, dealers are given exclusive access to a particular geographic area. The franchiser maintains control over whatever marketing methods are applied. In nearly all cases, the method, product, or service being marketed is identified by a brand name and often has uniform symbols, trademarks, and standardized services.

For the prospective home business person, franchising may be approached from two different angles. One could invest in an established franchise business and become a franchisee, or the home business person with a successful business could establish a franchise based on his or her business and recruit franchisees to start similar businesses in their homes. Let's examine each option.

Investing in a franchise

In order to operate a business as a franchise, one normally has to purchase the franchise from the owner. Many franchises such as hotels, restaurants, gas stations, and retail outlets are out of the realm of home business because they require standardized storefronts and may not be conducted from the home. However, there are a number of franchise businesses, usually owned by other home entrepreneurs, which may be operated at home.

When you purchase franchise rights to operate a home business, you are given licensed privilege to do business under the franchise name. Normally, you also receive assistance in setting up your business and are given details of methods to use in running that business. This instruction is commonly provided in a detailed manual. The franchiser may also be available for questions or problems you encounter.

Since buying into a franchise business will cost you a certain amount of investment capital and you will have to operate the business in the manner prescribed by the franchise owner, entering into any franchise agreement should be a carefully thought-out decision. Investigate the franchise thoroughly to determine whether it is a good investment for you. You may want to have an attorney look over the contract you are considering, as he or she can advise you of your rights and responsibilities under the agreement.

Evaluating a Franchise

When evaluating the merits of any particular franchise business, you may want to uncover the answers to these questions:

- How much equity capital will you need to acquire in order to purchase the franchise and operate it until you begin to show a profit? _____

  _____

  _____

- Does the franchise give you an exclusive territory, or can other franchises be sold in your area? ___

  _____

  _____

- How will the franchise firm assist you—with training programs, credit, capital, and/or merchandising ideas? _____

  _____

  _____

- What are the net profits of currently operating businesses within the franchise? (Check these figures with another franchisee if possible.) _____

  _____

  _____

- Under what circumstances can you terminate the franchise contract, and what is the cost to you if you wish to cancel it? _____

  _____

  _____

- Do you have the abilities and experience necessary to run the franchise profitably? _____

_____

_____

- What can the franchiser do for you that you can't do for yourself? _____

_____

_____

- Are you willing to give up a certain amount of independence in order to secure the advantages that the franchise offers? _____

_____

_____

- Is there a market in your area for the service (or product) which the franchise offers? _____

_____

_____

- How much competition exists in your area for the franchise you are contemplating? _____

_____

_____

Buying into a franchise business can offer a number of advantages, perhaps the most notable being consumer recognition and goodwill. However, there are also drawbacks such as loss of autonomy and reduced freedom for personal innovation. Carefully weigh the decision to purchase a franchise before committing yourself because most franchise contracts commit you for relatively long periods of time.

Franchising your home business

If you have a successful home business with unique or particularly saleable methods, products, and/or services, you may want to consider franchising your home business. You can sell franchises to people interested in starting their own home businesses. Presumably, you can pass on the fruits of your experience, methods with which you've achieved success, and your business name, which will give the franchise the reputation that you have already established.

For a home business franchiser, the most workable franchising method is to develop a franchise package. This should contain a manual that describes in detail how your service is performed or product is produced, methods of business, marketing techniques to be used, and any rules which should be adhered to in operating the business. You can also include the business logo, press release forms, and other materials that the franchiser will need to set up the business.

Based on the amount of control you want to retain, you and your attorney should draw up a contract detailing the rights and responsibilities of both of the involved parties. Remember that your business reputation will be affected by how your franchisees operate their businesses, so you may want to include a contract clause which specifies that failure to follow your rules will result in revocation of the franchisee's right to your business name and logo.

Keep in mind that anyone who considers investing in a franchise of your business will be looking for the advantages that the franchise will bring to them. Consequently, the amount of control you retain and responsibilities you place on the franchisee should be balanced with the amount of assistance and other advantages your franchise has to offer. Be realistic, also, in the amount of control you can actually retain; supervision of a number of franchises can be difficult and time consuming for one person.

One option you might consider is to sell your franchising package for a certain amount of money with no strings attached. In this manner, you will be able to make a profit in helping others start similar home businesses without having to deal with the work and responsibilities of supervising franchises. Buyers of your package will have the benefit of your knowledge and business experience and will still be able to maintain their autonomy. If you choose this option, you probably won't want to give people rights to your business name and logo since you will have no control over their business practices once they have purchased your package. Whatever approach you decide to use, carefully conceived franchising can be a profitable and gratifying venture for the home business entrepreneur.

Free-lancing

If you have talent as a writer, illustrator, or photographer, you may be able to develop a home business as a free-lancer. Many publications accept articles, artwork, and photographs from free-lance workers for use in their magazines and other publications. For most types of free-lancing, you are paid a flat rate for your work.

Writing   Hundreds of magazines, newspapers, and other publications use the works of free-lance authors. Free-lance writing is a highly competitive field, however, so it is very important that you have excellent writing skills in order to succeed in this business. Since most publications are looking for nonfiction pieces, a broad base of general knowledge and experience in researching topics is essential to the writer.

Most articles are written *on speculation.* This means that you write an article of a specified length on a certain topic. If the publication decides to use the article, they will pay you a predetermined rate. If they decide not to use it, you receive no compensation. After you have established a reputation as a writer, you may receive writing assignments *on acceptance.* In this case, you write an article on a specified topic and of a specified length. If the publication decides to use your article, you are paid the agreed amount. If they decide not to print it, you are paid a prearranged portion of the fee.

If you are at first unable to get assignments from any publications, you can try selling *unsolicited* material. You may write articles on topics that are interesting and in demand. Then, send the article to a number of publications in order to increase its chances of acceptance. Cover letters accompanying your work should describe the contents and approximate length of the article and give an address and phone number at which you can be reached if they are interested in using your piece.

In some cases it may be more desirable not to send your article in advance. In these instances, just send a letter describing the content of the article and its thrust or purpose as well as its length with appropriate information regarding how you can be reached. This approach will minimize the chances of your work being used without credit or payment to you.

While many publications do occasionally use unsolicited material, this is a difficult means of selling your work for at least two reasons:

- There is stiff competition among free-lance writers, and as a result, many publications are inundated with unsolicited material. With such an abundance of unsolicited articles, yours may never even be considered for publication. In fact, some magazines have a policy against using unsolicited pieces in order to avoid wading through hundreds of articles each month.

- In writing on a topic of your own choosing, you are less likely to meet the needs of a given publication at the time your article is received.

An established free-lancer may be offered particular assignments to cover. This is a more secure type of free-lance assignment; but unless you are known to be an expert in a particular topic area, such assignment offers may not be readily forthcoming.

The key to successful free-lance writing is persistence in trying to get your works published. Make as many contacts with publications as you can in an effort to get someone interested in having you write material for her or his publication. If an article is refused by one publication, try another; they might be willing to use it. Don't overlook smaller publications. There are literally hundreds of small newspapers and specialty magazines that may be interested in your work. You can also contact publications and try to get an assignment to write an article on a topic that they currently want to cover.

While you are trying to become established, you may even want to do a story or two without pay, so you can show other publications that your work has been published. As you have articles published, make a scrapbook of your published pieces to show other editors the quality of your work. The important thing is to keep trying, and remember that many syndicated columnists and other established writers began in much the same way.

Photography   Individuals skilled in photography have a number of options to earn money with their talent. One very common home business is wedding photography. You could also take portraits in your home. One of the most challenging and potentially lucrative alternatives is free-lance photography. Photographers will find that many varied markets exist for free-lance work.

Some of the same publications that employ the works of free-lance writers may also use photos taken by free-lance photographers. If you have unusual photographs or have the opportunity to shoot such photos, you can often market them to fill special needs of magazines, newspapers, other periodicals, and occasionally even books.

Photography agents and networks are common avenues for connecting those in need of a particular type of photo with photographers who have appropriate pictures to fulfill that need. For example, if some publication needs a photograph depicting a tornado touching down to earth and your photography agent knows that you have an appropriate photo, he or she will connect you with the publication so that you can sell them your picture. Photo networks work in much the same way, except that each photographer receives a full listing of all the photos being sought by every firm that uses the network. Actual contact with the publication is left up to the individual photographer in most cases.

As a photographer, you may also approach a publication directly to let them know the types of photos you have in your files and to leave samples of your work in order that they can determine its quality. You may be able to get assignments from a particular publication to take specific photographs to supplement news stories or magazine articles if they are aware of your skill with a camera.

Usually photographers are paid a set price for a photo or group of photos rather than fees based on a per-hour basis. The possible exception to this would be the coverage of expenses incurred if a publication sends you on assignment to get photographs of some particular event or place.

Aside from different types of publications, the free-lance photographer has many other outlets to which he or she can market photographs. Advertising agencies, marketing firms, design studios, film and slide studios, and large companies all employ the services of photographers. As a free-lancer, you may have the opportunity either to take pictures for the company's use or to provide them with existing photos that meet their needs. In order to sell your work in these types of markets, it will probably be necessary to show prospective clients samples of your work and to negotiate prices for your work, unless you are dealing through some kind of agent or broker.

Most photographers who prefer to do their own developing and printing build darkrooms in some area of their homes. The home-based free-lance photographer will also need an organized method of storing photographs and negatives or slides. Then, when the demand arises, a particular photograph can be located easily and reproduced in order to be shown and/or sold to a client. Other home office needs should be minimal; much of the actual photography will take place outside the home.

Illustration and commercial art

Artistic ability is the main prerequisite for free-lance illustrators and commercial artists. Markets do exist for free-lance illustrators, although they may not be quite as prevalent as markets for other types of free-lance work. Magazines, books, and children's books often use illustrations and are possible markets for a free-lance illustrator. Many magazines and other publications also use cartoons, if that is your specialty.

Methods for approaching potential clients are similar to those outlined for writers and photographers. Since illustrations are generally used in conjunction with stories or articles, you may find that seeking out authors who need illustrations for their works is another possible approach to selling your illustrations.

The field of commercial art is probably one of the best areas for the free-lance artist to find clients. Many small businesses require artwork for their ads, brochures, and other promotional materials. You can approach these businesses with samples of your work and offer to do art layouts for their advertisements. Advertising agencies and marketing firms may also be interested in using your services.

Free-lancing, whether in art, photography, writing, or other related areas, can prove to be a stimulating, personally rewarding type of business. A high degree of talent coupled with aggressive marketing can assure that it is also reasonably profitable.

You will need to research your market carefully before starting this particular kind of home business. Often, the successful free-lancer has worked in a particular metropolitan area for many years before "going free-lance." In that way the person has developed an ongoing relationship with, and knowledge of, a particular market. Having an agent, being an active member of professional associations in your area, and keeping up on news publications and other sources of information are all helpful steps in becoming a free-lancer.

Product
Businesses

7

Although home businesses may seem to some like a relatively new development in the working world, cottage industries were actually the most prevalent type of manufacturing prior to the Industrial Revolution, and they were quite common as recently as the early twentieth century. A cottage industry, as mentioned in an earlier chapter, traditionally consisted of an entrepreneur who purchased raw materials and paid home craftsmen for their labor in making a product. The entrepreneur then found a market for the finished product. Cottage workers were equivalent to independent contractors rather than employees. Today's home product businesses may be modeled after traditional cottage industries or structured like most current product businesses.

Producing Products   A wide variety of home businesses involves the production of a particular item. These businesses may make custom designs for one-of-a-kind products, take orders for a limited number of products, or mass-produce one particular item.

Some product businesses are begun as an outgrowth of a hobby. You may have an idea for a product that seems like a good idea to you and that is not currently available on the market. Ideas such as these have been the beginning of numerous successful home businesses. Snuggli™ baby carriers started out as a home business when a new mother wanted a hands-free way of carrying her baby but could find nothing on the market to fulfill her needs. Her mother designed a cloth baby carrier, and a successful business was born.

Ideas to improve already available products can also provide the means to a lucrative product business. Nearly any type of product can be the basis for a successful home business, as long as there is a definite market for the product and the entrepreneur is able to produce the goods in a cost-effective manner. Customers may pay slightly more for a product that is better made or has an unusual feature compared to others available; but if your production costs do not allow your goods to be competitively priced, it is unlikely that you will be successful in marketing your product.

Do I Have a Good Product?

1. Describe the product you plan to make. _____

_____

_____

2. Are there similar products currently on the market? If so, how well do they do on the market? _____

_____

_____

_____

3. How is your product an improvement over what is currently available? Be specific. Does it do the job more effectively? Cost less to operate? Save the customer time or money? Is it more attractive? More durable? _____

_____

_____

_____

4. What is the reaction of friends and acquaintances to your product? _____

_____

_____

_____

_____

5. How can you fine-tune or improve your product? _____

_____

_____

_____

Number of workers   When first starting a home-based production venture, most businesses have only one or two employees. For certain types of custom businesses such as jewelry making, cabinetry, and custom weaving, a small volume of business may be enough to provide a living; and there may be no need or desire to add other employees. In other cases where a product business grows to such proportions that the owner is unable to keep up with product demand, two alternatives are available.

Hiring helpers. You may decide to hire employees to assist you in your business. Before you take this step, however, make sure you can afford it. Hiring extra help should be an action that increases your business income rather than depletes your resources. If this approach is used, you must make sure to take care of such things as workmen's compensation and payroll withholdings. You will also have to determine whether your employees will work in your home or in their own homes. In either case, you should consult your local zoning laws and state laws, because they may restrict business size or limit who may work in a given home enterprise.

Some home business owners select their extra helpers very casually. They often hire neighbors, friends, or family members who express an interest in helping out with the business. While this works satisfactorily for some, it is usually better to use a more stringent selection process in order to assure yourself the best workers you can. Your neighbor may seem interested in helping you produce your dolls; but if the neighbor doesn't sew well, hiring that person might prove to be a costly mistake.

Anyone who has applied for a job knows the often rigorous procedures which traditional employers use in choosing new employees. Application forms, résumés, aptitude and psychological tests, and interviews are just some of the tools used to screen applicants before a final decision is made. It is not necessary to use such a formal screening process as this; however, as a home business person you would probably benefit from using at least one or more of these tools. Whatever method you employ, be sure to find out the following information from anyone you consider hiring or using as a subcontractor:

- Does the applicant have the skills that are required to do the job?

- What kind of applicable experience does the prospective employee possess?

- Is the applicant a reliable, industrious, and honest worker? (Previous employment records will usually reflect this information.)

- What kind of wage or fee is the prospective worker seeking? Is it in line with what you are prepared to offer?

- What kind of commitment is the applicant willing to make to your business? How many hours per week is he or she available for work? Does the person view the job as temporary or longer range?

With the above information at hand, you should be able to make a well-informed choice of employees. Careful screening will lessen frequent employee turnover and aid you in choosing good workers who will be a benefit to your business operation.

Subcontracting. A second approach to large-scale home production is patterned after the traditional cottage industry model. You may subcontract part of the work to other people wishing to work in their own homes. These subcontractors would make your product, using your designs or specifications, and they would be paid in the same way as you would pay any other subcontractor.

Establishing a cottage industry that incorporates the labor of others in this manner can be complicated. It is extremely important that you get expert legal advice before you expand your cottage industry so that you are aware of all the federal requirements for home businesses. Keeping careful records of your business is important to show the Internal Revenue Service that you are, in actuality, meeting these federal requirements.

Concerns unique to product businesses

While the basics of running a home enterprise apply to any type of business, product businesses present some areas of concern which are not applicable to service businesses. Consideration of these unique factors can help assure your business success. By analyzing them fully during the business planning stage, many early failures that plague small businesses might be averted.

Purchasing materials. Purchasing supplies can pose problems for the small product business since it is often difficult to buy small quantities of supplies at anything less than retail prices. To avoid this, you might try to get together with two or three other small businesses who need the same supplies in order to get a minimum order from a wholesaler of supplies. Professional organizations or informal networks may provide you with the needed contacts.

Packaging. Product businesses need to carefully consider packaging and shipping, if the products are sold by mail order, and other costs associated with getting the product distributed to whatever or wherever your market is. Packaging should be designed or selected to protect the product, and the packaging should have a professional look. Preferably it should also promote your product by having either your business name or logo displayed.

Pricing. A myriad of factors must be considered in setting the price for your product. Don't overlook design, supplies, construction, packaging, shipping, marketing expenses, and most importantly, your own time.

Many craftspersons drastically undervalue their time and consequently undercharge for their products. If providing yourself with a reasonable wage for your time causes your price to be too high to be competitive, you may need to find other ways to cut production costs. If this is impossible, you should face the fact that the product is not a profitable one for you to produce. You need to find some other product that will be profitable for you.

Special Product Considerations

	Cost per Unit	Suppliers/Notes
Raw Materials		
Packaging		
Labeling		
Labor		
Postage or Delivery Costs		

Food products. Food products may also be made in the home although there are more government restrictions regarding health and sanitary standards for the manufacture of any food product than for other types of product businesses. Therefore, when contemplating the production of a food product, be sure to check your local and state laws.

Generally, specialty or gourmet foods are the most profitable types of food for a home business to produce. Such foods can be sold at a higher price and require lower sales volume to make a profit. If the food is capable of being stored for some period of time, such as fruitcakes, preserves, sausages, or candy, you may be able to do a mail order business.

Gourmet food shops provide another outlet for food products. You can approach stores with samples of your product and, hopefully, take away orders to supply them with your merchandise. You can also approach caterers and even restaurants. Specialty items such as decorated cakes, cheesecakes, or candy may also be sold directly to the public in your area.

Product liability. A critical aspect of manufacturing a product from home is the extent to which a business owner is liable for injury or damage caused by the product's use. Product liability is potentially one of the most serious of all business liabilities. It is increasingly common for courts to hold the manufacturer, and sometimes the seller, almost totally responsible for injury or property damage due to a defective or unsafe product when used as intended. Misrepresenting the character or quality of a product through advertising is also liable activity if it causes injury or damage.

It is extremely important to be well-informed about product liability law, product safety design, causes of product failures, and product liability cost estimation. In light of these facts, any home entrepreneur engaged in the manufacture of a product would be well advised to investigate product liability insurance.

Copyrights and patents. A worksteader with a unique product should also be concerned with copyrights and patents. This is another area of business for which legal advice is strongly recommended.

If you want to protect your ideas or designs, you need copyright protection. Without a copyright, anyone can use your idea or design, and you have no legal protection or recourse. Copyrights will protect products of original design, such as games, dolls, and patterns, as well as written works.

Generally, you have to take dated pictures of your product and write a description of it, detailing those things that make it unique. While it is possible to obtain copyrights on your own, it is generally better to let a legal firm experienced in copyright matters handle the process of establishing your copyrights.

If you have actually invented a new "gizmo" or "widget," you need to consider applying for a patent. A patent is granted for a new invention. A patent gives the inventor the right to exclude others from making, using, or selling the invention for a specified period of time. Patents apply only within the United States.

A patent is granted upon providing a complete description of a new machine, manufactured article, chemical-type compound, or industrial-technical process. Patents are not granted for ideas, marketing strategies, or original designs of existing products. Patent law stipulates that, "A new and useful process, machine, manufacture or composition of matter, or any new and useful improvements thereof may obtain a patent. . . ."

While you will probably want legal assistance in obtaining a patent, the following general guidelines will show how and when you can obtain a patent:

- Evaluate the invention to determine whether or not it is really a marketable improvement over existing products.

- Get someone you trust to sign his or her name on a dated diagram of the invention.

- Make a patent search to see whether your invention has already been patented or whether a better product already exists.

- If the invention has not been patented, prepare a patent application and file it with the U.S. Patent and Trademark Office.

If you make any changes in the invention, you should, of course, promptly notify the patent office.

Selling Products

After goods have been produced by a home business, they have to be sold. The type of marketing strategy will be affected by the type of product, the type of market the product appeals to, and the availability of sale outlets. Other factors such as the personal preference of the home business operator may also figure into marketing strategies. By dint of necessity, marketing strategies of home business people are often more creative than their traditional business counterparts.

Marketing is the key to most small businesses. Don't be afraid to look at new and unique ways of reaching your customers. The least expensive way is to have your customers come to your home to purchase and pick up your product (or service). Or, you can adapt marketing ideas from chapter 5. Remember that there are many other ways of getting the job done if one method isn't practical for either you or the majority of your potential customers.

Direct sales   For some products in the home, selling directly to the public from your home is a possibility. This works especially well for custom-made products wherein each product is made specifically to order for a customer. Furniture, cabinetry, and stained glass works are just a few examples of possible made-to-order products.

Even if your products are not made to order, selling from your home may work if you have a small area of your home which can be designated as your "store." In this case, in addition to word-of-mouth contact with buyers, you will probably need to do some outside advertising to alert customers to your business and its location.

Mail order   One very common outlet for home-produced items is the mail-order business. To sell products by mail order, the business owner advertises the products for sale to potential customers. Interested parties respond to the ad by sending payment for the product through the mail. The product is then shipped directly to the customer's home. Basically, two means of advertising are commonly used in mail-order businesses, media advertising and direct mail.

Media advertising. One method of attracting customers for your mail-order business is through media outlets. You can either place ads in magazines, on radio or television, or in newspapers and then have interested parties respond to your ads. Normally, entrepreneurs who place ads in publications select those which attract people likely to buy their particular products. If you make tool caddies, for example, a magazine for mechanics would obviously be better than a fashion magazine. Selecting this method of advertising your mail order business is probably preferable if you produce one or only a few products.

Direct mail. If your business has a number of products or if the products require some description or pictures in order to be appreciated and purchased, the direct-mail approach may be more advantageous than advertising through mass media. Here the business person makes up a brochure, advertisement, or small catalog that is mailed to a number of potential customers.

Direct mail is often more cost effective than advertising in a large publication for several reasons. First, people may miss an ad in a magazine, but they are less likely to overlook a piece of mail sent directly to their homes. Second, as the home business person develops a mailing list, he or she will be reaching those people who have a definite interest in the product. Third, although the initial cost of developing a brochure can be expensive, it is often less expensive in the long run than placing ads in a major publication.

The direct-mail approach depends on mailing lists, which were discussed at some length in chapter 5. Lists of names and addresses can be purchased from mailing list companies that have broken down their lists according to interests and demographics, so the business person is more likely to reach people who would be interested in buying a particular product. Whether or not you initially use a rented list, be sure to start your own list based on past customers and other people who have made inquiries.

Retail outlets   Another method of marketing is to sell your product to a retail store or to sell it through a retail store on consignment. In certain instances, you may even be able to lease some space in a store where you can sell your product. In all three of these instances, it is necessary to contact retail outlets in the area with samples of your product and to persuade the store managers that your product will sell well in their stores. You may agree to have a store take items on a trial basis to determine whether or not there is a market for your product among their clientele.

Some cooperative stores are ideally set up for the home business entrepreneur. Mainly craft stores, these co-ops are generally run by a group of people with products they'd like to sell. Each member donates time to tend the shop, and all members can sell their products from that outlet.

Be creative   Other possible ways to sell cottage industry items include craft fairs and expositions, home shows or parties, and even telephone or door-to-door sales. Creativity is especially important in marketing home business goods. Remember that while one method of sales may work for you at one time, you may find that a combination of marketing strategies works best. As the business grows, you may also discover that the most profitable methods of sales may change. Therefore, it's important to remain flexible about marketing techniques. Be open to new methods; and if one method isn't working to your satisfaction, don't be afraid to try something else.

Remember that your creativity must begin with your product. To gain a competitive edge, the product you make should have something distinctive or some quality that is unavailable in commercially made products. The product can be new and otherwise unavailable, as in gourmet doggy treats or unusual clothing or equipment for babies; or the product should have its own individual twist that sets it apart from what is generally available. Nearly any product can be made at home, but what you choose to produce should be adapted to your own interests, special talents, and above all, the people you see as your customers. A well-made, needed product will make selling a much easier task.

Hiring sales representatives

Since finding markets for home-produced goods is such a time-consuming task, you may find it advantageous to hire a sales representative for your product line. A sales representative is different from a salesperson in that a sales representative gets orders for your goods but does not directly sell your product as a salesperson would.

Sales representatives take samples of your product to stores, gift and trade shows, and other potential outlets for your goods. They take orders from clients that they then forward to you to fill. The customers pay you directly for the goods you send them. You pay your sales rep a commission based on a percentage of the dollar amount of the orders he or she gets for you.

The selection of your sales representative is an important decision, since the success of your business is reliant on a healthy volume of sales. For this reason, make sure that anyone you choose as a sales rep is familiar with the type of products you produce. Familiarity with your product and its most saleable points will help to ensure that the sales representative can present your goods most effectively. Any representative you use should be enthusiastic about your product because this attitude will be conveyed to prospective clients.

For any type of business, there are good sales representatives and bad ones. Be wary of sales representatives who want to receive the cash for your orders and then forward it to you. You may have difficulty getting your money in a timely fashion, or even at all, if the sales rep is truly dishonest. You also want to make sure that your sales representative is willing to really work for you by visiting many stores and trade shows. You should be able to tell in a matter of a few months whether or not the sales rep you have selected is really putting effort into selling your product.

As the manufacturer, you also have several responsibilities to your sales representative. Keep in close communication to keep him or her up-to-date on new product lines, product changes, price changes, and the amount of time it will take to fill an order. Make sure that you fill orders by the promised date, so that your sales rep can maintain a good relationship with clients in the field. Also make sure that you pay your sales representative's commission promptly. After all, it's hard to remain enthusiastic about promoting a product line if you aren't getting paid promptly for the work that you are doing.

Working in Sales

Another home business that you might consider is sales. While many product businesses involve producing and then selling a product, there are several other selling alternatives that do not involve the production of a product.

If you consider this possibility, remember that most sales jobs that you can do from home require a certain amount of storage space for inventory. Be sure that you have the facilities for this type of venture.

Direct sales companies

There are a number of companies that use direct sales forces, the majority of which work from home. You are probably familiar with several of these companies including Avon, Tupperware, Watkins Products, and others involving a wide range of products including toys, housewares, cosmetics, lingerie, and jewelry. Many of these companies offer training programs for their salespeople, who usually work on commission. Salespeople may sell by having prospective customers come to their homes, going door-to-door, or presenting products at home parties hosted by customers, who receive incentive gifts for inviting friends to their homes to examine the product and listen to a short demonstration by the salesperson.

Direct sales positions such as these often make ideal part-time ventures. In most cases, you initially have to purchase a demonstration kit in order to become a salesperson for the company, but the investment is usually reasonably small. Depending on the company, there may be room for advancement. Such advancement is usually based on the recruitment of new salespeople, volume of sales, or both. If you are able to devote substantial time and persistent effort to such a position, it can be quite profitable.

Importing   An interesting sales alternative is starting an import business from your home. If you do any traveling and come across products not readily available in the United States, you can make arrangements to import the product for resale. Imported goods can be sold by mail order, direct to customers, or to retail stores.

Importing goods requires that certain import tariffs be paid, so your profit margin must allow for this added cost as well as for shipping. Some goods have restrictions on their importation into this country, so you will need to check with the federal government to see if your particular product has any restrictions. There may be other legal considerations as well, depending on the product, so consult your attorney before investing in an import business.

Retail sales   Depending on the size and zoning of your home, retail sales may be a possible type of home business venture. Several types of retail outlets are particularly well suited to home operation. Antique stores, gift shops, art galleries, boutiques, clothing resale shops, and toy stores are just a few types of retail stores that can be operated successfully from your home.

Such an enterprise, of course, requires that some portion of your home be devoted to the store; and ideally, the area should be clearly separated from your living quarters. A room or several rooms with separate outside access and doors closing off the rest of the house would be suitable. If the house is large enough, you might consider devoting a whole floor of your house to the business.

After selecting the type of store you would like to run, you purchase your goods from wholesalers, local craftspeople, or, in the case of antique shops, estate sales, auctions, and similar sales. If you are selling art or craft items, you may take items on consignment or purchase them outright for resale. For other types of businesses, you will need to rely on wholesale suppliers. Many wholesalers require that you place large orders, so you may have to shop around for a supplier who meets your needs or place a joint order with two or three other businesses carrying similiar merchandise.

Mail-order sales   Mail-order businesses are discussed in other sections of this book; nevertheless, it is important to point out that you can run a mail-order home business with goods someone else has produced. Methods for obtaining these goods would generally be the same as those for running a store.

In order to make this type of mail-order business profitable, it is usually best to sell a number of items rather than specialize with a single product. In this way, customers have more selection and repeat business is more likely.

You will need space enough in your home for your inventory and for processing and packaging your orders. Check with the post office for their rules concerning mail-order businesses. You can either rent a post office box for your business or use your home address. Many people place more confidence in a business with a permanent street address.

Wholesale businesses

As unlikely as it may seem, it is also possible to run a wholesale business from your home. Wholesaling is acting as a middleman; you buy from one company and sell to another. Or you can buy large quantities of items from craftspeople or home product manufacturers and sell to other firms. Instead of selling to individual consumers, you sell large orders to other businesses, most commonly retail outlets.

Generally, there are no special laws governing wholesale businesses, but you should check with an attorney or state officials to determine local and state requirements. The Small Business Administration has literature available on running small wholesale firms that may prove useful if you are contemplating this type of enterprise.

The Electronic Cottage

In the work-at-home world, a computerized work site is commonly referred to as an *electronic cottage*. This term, coined by Alvin Toffler, has come to mean any computerized work station in the home. It includes both self-employment ventures and remote work site arrangements set up by more traditional companies. The electronic cottage has contributed much to the resurgence of home business in the United States.

In the last two decades we've seen the development of hand-held programmable calculators, portable computer terminals, and word processing equipment that can be operated at home to generate printouts both at home and at the office. Facsimile and electronic mail equipment, portable dictating machines, video recorders, and telecommuting equipment have also become quite commonplace. These and other technological developments are helping to make many home businesses more efficient and economical and, thereby, practical alternatives to traditional work arrangements.

Until the advent of microcomputers and related technological advances, the decentralization of business was simply not a practical alternative to centralized work sites which assured effective communication between workers. The availability of small, affordable microcomputers and telecommunication systems has changed all that.

Now it is not only possible but also often economically advantageous to have workers at decentralized work stations. In an age in which both time and fuel are precious commodities, telecommuting from home sites is economically sound for both the employer and the worker.

The mass of affordable, easy-to-use home computers has also, for the first time, made it feasible for small cottage industries to bring computers into their operations. Just ten or fifteen years ago the sheer size and cost of computers would have made this alternative practically impossible.

Often referred to as *home computers*, most computers marketed for home use, with the exception of those intended primarily for video games, are more accurately called *personal computers* or *PCs*. Many home businesses have been affected by the rapid proliferation of PCs. In fact, several surveys have shown that most personal computers found in residences are used for educational and/or business purposes. As they become even more commonplace—given the rapid growth of computer technology—computers should be even more accessible to small home businesses in the next few years.

Types of Computer Work

The use of computers at home for employment purposes can be broadly divided into two categories. For our purposes, we'll call the first category telecommuting businesses and refer to the second group as computerized home businesses.

The main difference between the two is that in *telecommuting,* the home worker is generally employed by an outside company. *Computerized home businesses,* on the other hand, refer to cottage industries that use computers in their work. While there may be some overlap, keeping this distinction in mind will facilitate discussion of these two types of electronic cottages.

Telecommuting Advances in computer technology have made it possible for employees to work outside the centralized office and still remain interactive with the office personnel, equipment, and data. As such, microcomputers have introduced telecommuting as a viable home work option.

In telecommuting, an employee works for a company by using a computer terminal set up in his or her home. This terminal is linked by means of a computer modem to the company's central computer. With such an arrangement, whatever work the employee does at home can be directly transmitted to the company's central office.

In recent years about two hundred corporations in various parts of the country have initiated telecommuting test programs in which they have installed computer systems in employees' homes. Most of these test programs have proven quite successful. Productivity is often higher for telecommuters than for traditional office workers performing the same kind of work. Employees gain various personal advantages, including not having to commute to the office every day. As these test programs become a permanent part of corporate operations and as more companies become involved, there will undoubtedly be growth in the telecommuting job market.

Frequently, telecommuters spend some portion of their work time at the central office. Employees may spend one or two days each week in the office in order to attend meetings with other employees and to do other work that requires face-to-face interaction with coworkers or clients.

As an alternative to work stations in the home, a number of *electronic neighborhood centers* have also been established by some companies in the last few years. These centers contain various types of computers and other office equipment not practical to have in one's home. Instead of driving all the way to the central office, employees drive a few miles to the neighborhood center where necessary office equipment is available for their use. Such neighborhood centers will no doubt play a part in greater use of flexi-time or flexi-place arrangements as work weeks in the future are divided between home, office, and electronic neighborhood centers.

Pros and cons of telecommuting

For the Telecommuter:

Pros	Cons
Offers more flexible hours and working conditions.	May lose some employee benefits, depending on the company.
Eliminates daily commuting and the associated expenses.	May be harder to make career advancement.
Lowers work-related expenses (lunches, working wardrobe, child care).	May feel cut off from co-workers.
Allows people with disabilities and those caring for young children or the infirm to continue working.	

For the Employer:

Pros	Cons
Receives higher productivity, both in terms of quantity and quality of work.	May feel it is difficult to adequately supervise telecommuters.
Requires less expense in terms of maintaining office space.	Are unanswered questions as to liability for accidents and equipment damage.
May lower training costs and employee turnover by keeping employees who might otherwise have to quit.	

Telecommuting jobs. Many different types of work can be done using telecommuting technology, or decentralizing computer systems. Experts on telecommuting point out that jobs which are considered ideal for telecommuting should share several characteristics:

- The work should be portable in terms of the resources needed to perform the job.

- The work should consist of well-defined, measurable tasks.

- The work situation requires minimal and predictable need for face-to-face interpersonal contact.

Clearly, a wide range of traditional office work falls within these guidelines.

Let's look at a few examples of jobs currently being done by telecommuting. Many mail-order catalog companies have phone orders placed with employees working from home terminals. Hotel reservations and telephone answering services for 800 numbers can be handled in much the same manner. Data processing, insurance claims, billing, and payrolls also are done efficiently through telecommuting. Other job categories include, but are not limited to, the following: technical writing, documentation writing, computer programming, data analysis, preparation of reports, and certain types of research. From this list it becomes clear that some aspects of nearly every office job can be done by telecommuting.

Telecommuting drawbacks. While telecommuting is gradually gaining wider acceptance, skeptics point out several disadvantages to this work alternative. Difficulties in effective management and isolation of telecommuting employees are the most frequently cited problems.

People in managerial positions worry about how they can effectively supervise employees that they rarely see. This problem can be overcome through greater use of telephone contacts and other measures to assure that the home worker receives adequate direction and feedback. Measuring an employee's performance, whether in the office or at home, should be looked at in terms of the quality and quantity of work performed rather than concentrated on personal supervision. Also, it should be recognized that most telecommuters spend at least a portion of their work week in the central office, so managers do have the opportunity to interact with these employees regularly.

As in other home work, isolation of telecommuters can be a serious problem. Candidates for this type of work must be self-starters who work well independently.

As much as possible, employers should help telecommuters feel part of the social and informational network of the office. Telecommuters should be sent memos, reports, and other information received by central office employees and included in formal office functions such as staff meetings and informal functions such as luncheons or company teams.

Concerns about liability for worker accidents and equipment damage are more difficult to resolve. If an employee is injured while working at home or if equipment in the home is damaged, who will be responsible—the employee or the company? At this point the question has not been satisfactorily resolved. Perhaps as telecommuting becomes a more established part of the business world, companies will recognize the need to resolve these issues.

Although these problems and others not mentioned do exist, telecommuting is a practical work alternative. The advantages of lower office costs, higher productivity, and a more personally satisfying life-style make telecommuting attractive for a significant number of both employers and employees. Opportunities in telecommuting will undoubtedly grow in the coming years. Microcomputers and telecommuting may well prove to be the most significant factors in the growth of the work-at-home movement.

Computerized home businesses

Computerized home businesses are an important part of the electronic cottage movement, and they more closely fit the traditional concept of cottage industries than their counterpart, telecommuting. Many computerized home businesses actually provide some type of computer service, while other home businesses simply use the personal computer as a tool to help them run their ventures more smoothly, efficiently, and professionally.

Computer service businesses. Computer service businesses include word processing, bookkeeping, and businesses that keep mailing lists or records for clients. Also in this category are data-base research services, computer consultants, and programmers.

Word processing is probably the most popular computer service being offered out of private homes. It can encompass a wide range of services including straight typing; typing and editing services; typing and document storage; preparation of newsletters or bulletins for businesses, churches, clubs, or associations; and production of handbooks, directories, manuals, or pamphlets. Many small businesses, which do not require full-time word processors, hire these services to take care of special projects or reports, an excellent opportunity for a home business, as many worksteaders have discovered.

Specialized knowledge can be highly useful for the home computer service. Law firms, for example, like to deal with people who are already familiar with the forms and jargon they use. If you have special expertise and this type of business appeals to you, begin by researching potential customers.

Computers in home businesses. For those who are not interested in running a computer service business, a computer can still be a very beneficial part of a home enterprise. Many people who think about using a personal computer come up with the same question, "If I buy a computer, what exactly could I do with it?" The answer is, "Just about anything!" Granted, there are still tasks that can be more efficiently done by hand than on a computer; but for the most part, nearly every office function can be carried out on a computer.

In putting computers to work, small companies often make two common and interrelated mistakes, computerizing what should remain a manual function and leaving as manual what would benefit most from computerization. Things that are not subject to change may not be best computerized. Things which are complex, changing, and/or interrelated benefit most from being computerized.

Computers seem to do best exactly those tasks which for a person are the most tedious and time consuming. Calculations of projected sales for next year, typing "personal" letters to fifty clients, addressing envelopes for everyone on your mailing list—each of these tasks would be time-consuming drudgery if done manually.

A computer can do the same jobs more accurately and in less time. More important, the time you save can be spent doing productive, creative work. It's easy to see how this would be a benefit to most small businesses.

Does Your Business Need a Computer?

Answer the following questions Yes or No. The more frequently you answer Yes, the more your business would benefit from a computer.

_____   My business would benefit by being able to access and transmit information from one computer to another.

_____   My business requires that I keep complex, frequently changing, or interrelated records.

_____   My business requires that I calculate complex projections or spreadsheets.

_____   My business deals with a great deal of information that needs to be stored and quickly retrieved.

_____   My business requires that I send a lot of "personalized" letters or other correspondence.

_____   My business involves repetitive, time-consuming typing or record keeping that could be done more efficiently on a computer.

Selecting the Right Computer

Computers can be divided into categories on the basis of whether they are designed for general applications or special applications. *General applications computers* are those which can be programmed by the owner to suit a variety of needs. Such computers are advantageous in that one basic computer can be tailored to fit multiple needs simply by changing or adding programs. Often these computers are designed and produced with built-in provisions for expansion. You can add new capabilities, such as extra memory, as they are needed simply by installing circuit boards into the appropriate slots.

Special applications computers are designed for a limited set of operations that are not easily modified by the owner. Examples of special-purpose microcomputers include video games, automated teller machines, and electronic cash registers. While there are obviously valuable applications for special-purpose computers, general applications computers are more useful to the home business person and are the main focus of this section.

All microcomputers produced today can be further divided into two basic groups. The first group is made up of computers which are geared to home and hobby use. The other group consists of computers designed primarily for business or industrial use.

Even though you might think that a microcomputer designed for business use would be the most appropriate computer choice for a home business, this is not usually the case. Microcomputers marketed for home use, if carefully selected, generally have all the capabilities required to make them useful in a home business.

If you have special needs, peripheral equipment—such as laser printers, modems, extra disk drives, and hard disks—expands the utility of a home computer. Whatever peripherals may be needed for your business applications, versions are generally available that are compatible with most personal computers. Purchasing the entire home computer package, including all the required peripherals, is considerably less expensive than the price of a microcomputer system marketed for business use.

Business computers are usually higher priced than home computers for several reasons:

- Business computers receive heavier use and hence need to be extremely well constructed and reliable.

- Business computer companies often supply support assistance to their customers, adding to the overhead costs that must be passed on to the business consumer.

- Many business applications require very large data storage capabilities, fast access to data, and rapid printout capabilities.

- Most business computer systems are sold as "bundled systems." This means that software, consulting, training, service and support contracts, and hardware are sold as a package.

- The extra cost is justified on the basis of potential savings (salaries, time).

Many business/industrial microcomputer systems can also be leased; whereas with personal computers, this is not ordinarily an available option. Clearly, business systems do offer more to their customers than do personal computers. However, these features are usually unnecessary and generally not worth the large price difference to the average home business owner.

There is a great deal of overlap in the capabilities of business and home use computers, particularly since personal computers continue to be improved and are built with increased capabilities. It is not uncommon for the same company to produce both business-oriented computers and home computers. It is also increasingly common to find computers marketed for home use in small business applications. For most home business applications, a personal computer is more than adequate.

Since a computer system represents a significant outlay of cash for most home enterprises, it is to your advantage to delay your computer purchase until you've decided exactly how you will use it. Initially, you may want to buy or borrow books and magazines to familiarize yourself with possible computer uses, different hardware and software options, and the potential advantages of expansion capabilities and peripherals. You may even hire a computer consultant to help you make your selection, including recommendations on the right combination of hardware and software for the needs of the business. Then start the process of actually shopping for your computer. Only after careful study and research should you make your final selection and purchase your equipment.

Selecting the Best Computer for Your Needs

Fill out this worksheet. Then, take it along to computer dealers and consultants so that they can match you with a system that will best meet your needs.

What are the demands of your particular business?
Specifically, what do you plan to do with your computer? (Type letters, keep inventory records, do cost analysis, keep accounts, do desk-top publishing?)

_____

_____

_____

What peripheral equipment, if any, will be necessary for the performance of your business tasks?
Will you need to communicate with other computer systems?

_____

How much information will you need to store? _____

_____

What quality of printing is necessary for your purposes? Do you need letter quality? Color printing? Laser quality?

_____

_____

Will you need expanded capabilities in the future?
Will you need more storage capacity? _____

_____

What other future needs do you see? _____

_____

_____

What amount of money can you afford to spend? _____

_____

Determining the answers to the above questions and discussing the matter with a well-informed computer salesperson will usually provide you with an idea of your best options. Make a point of comparison shopping. Since computer stores generally deal in only one or a few brand names, they are not likely to recommend a competing computer, even if it might better suit your needs.

Another advantage of comparison shopping is that you will become more knowledgeable about what is available and thus better able to make a well-informed choice. And, perhaps just as important, you may be able to save a significant amount of money by seeing what different retail outlets have to offer.

Selecting Software

After having familiarized yourself with your personal computer, you will have to acquire the appropriate software to do the task you desire. Walking into a software store for the first time can be an overwhelming experience. You simply wanted to be able to type letters on your PC, and there are thirty different word processing packages staring you in the face! Just knowing what you need can be a challenge.

Software packages are available to do an almost unbelievably wide variety of tasks. There are programs currently available that allow you to do bookkeeping and keep tax records, keep track of inventory, project sales and profits, write personalized form letters, send billing notices on your own letterhead, keep mailing lists, and write letters, press releases, and articles which can be saved and altered for later use.

Programs are also available that allow you to file and retrieve information and check what you've written for spelling and grammatical errors. There are even graphics programs you can use to design flyers and other materials to promote your business.

When selecting software, you should keep several things in mind:

- First, make sure the program has a well-written, comprehensive manual. Since you are likely to be dependent on the manual to explain every feature and nuance of the program, a good manual is just as important as the program itself.

- Second, compare software to make sure that the program you select *actually* performs the tasks that you need to have done. If you need a program that allows you to make pie graphs, for instance, make sure the program has the capability to make pie graphs.

- A third important consideration is ease of use. While two software packages may carry out basically the same functions, one may be considerably easier for a person to use. Obviously, a user-friendly program is preferable to one that is difficult to use.

How can you be sure a program is just what you need? Computer magazines often carry reviews of software packages that describe a program's capabilities and rate its quality. Good stores, another source of help, will be able to make recommendations of software based on your described needs.

Some stores may also let you try a software package in the store, although this isn't always the case. Since business packages are often expensive, you should request to have the software demonstrated before you buy it. If a store refuses to do so, try another store. If at all possible, try to use a program yourself before you buy it. At the very least, get recommendations from people who have experience with that type of program.

Be aware that over-the-counter software is purchased as is and offers no guarantee that it will perform the functions necessary for your applications. Such software is generally not returnable, so make sure a program is what you need before you make your purchase.

New software is constantly becoming available. It's not difficult to find commercial programs to fill almost every business need. If you are already skilled in computer programming or as you gain experience, you may be able to modify or write a custom program to fit your precise needs. There are even books and magazines available that can help you do this.

Special skills and training

Few computer buyers can simply plug in their units and get down to business. Most people will need some kind of training. The skills you need to use the computer effectively depend largely on three major factors:

- The type of work you are doing.

- The type of computer you have.

- The software program you will use.

Type of work

In evaluating the type of work you are doing, the level of difficulty and the complexity of the task or tasks determine the special skills and training you will need. For example, computer programming, whether developing new programs or modifying existing ones, obviously requires more skill and training than simply using a word processing program.

Generally, if you are considering a career in computer operating and/or programming, you should plan to get training in computers at a business training school or a technical or vocational school at the very least. If you are seriously interested in becoming a programmer, a four-year college program in computer science or some related area is usually necessary.

Work in computer-based service businesses will require a fair amount of expertise in working with computers, although such work may not require quite as much knowledge of computers as programming and other highly technical computer fields. While formal training for these types of service businesses and other computerized home businesses isn't generally required, or widely available for that matter, informal training for the particular computer and software to be used should be undertaken by the entrepreneur. The business section of many newspapers regularly lists business-related courses and seminars, including computer training, available in the area.

In addition to the technical knowledge and skills needed to use a computer and software, it is important that the home business person have knowledge and training in the particular area of application as well. To illustrate, if a person is using a program intended to aid architects in drawing plans for a building, he or she must, of course, have knowledge and training in the field of architecture in addition to knowledge of the computer and software being used.

Requiring considerably less computer knowledge and fewer skills would be the home business person who is using a personal computer to keep relatively simple business records or to print form letters. However, since some experience or education is necessary, you should take advantage of whatever training is available to you. Some avenues of training for use of personal computers and software are discussed further in the following sections of this chapter.

Sources of computer training

- Local colleges and universities

- Technical/vocational schools

- Business training schools

- Business/computer seminars (Look in the business section of your local newspaper.)

- Continuing or adult education courses (May be offered through colleges, technical schools, and/or high schools.)

- Classes offered by computer dealers

- Computer consultants

- Tutoring from knowledgeable friends or acquaintances

- Computer manuals

- Software documentation

- Other books on computers

- Computer magazines

Type of computer It also stands to reason that the more complex a computer is, the more special training will be required to operate it. For certain types of telecommuters and other workers who may be using some of the more sophisticated computers, special training is usually necessary.

Companies sometimes train their own employees in the use of the particular computers that they use, or they may send employees to training seminars. Of course, companies usually expect employees to have some computer experience or training before they are hired. Company training then focuses on familiarizing the employee with the company's particular computer and programs.

Most home business people are probably not interested in delving into computers in such depth. They want to be able to use personal computers either as the basis of service businesses or to streamline the efficiency of their businesses.

Happily, learning to use the majority of home or personal computers is a relatively simple matter. Depending on where you buy your computer, you may find you have an excellent learning resource in your computer dealer. Computer dealers are usually eager to teach you about their products and to match you with a computer that suits your needs. In fact, many computer dealers offer classes, either free or for a small fee, to teach you how to use your new PC.

If your computer store doesn't offer such courses, there are a number of other possible resources you can check. Most vocational and technical schools offer introductory courses in computer use, as do university continuing education programs. Your local high school may also offer computer courses as part of its regular or adult education programs.

User groups are another excellent source of help in learning to use a particular computer. Usually organized on the basis of the type of computer which all of its members own, such a group can help you to solve particular problems you have in operating your computer or in using particular software packages on it.

Don't overlook the possibility of tutoring from a friend or acquaintance who is knowledgeable about computers. Often such one-on-one experience is just what's needed to help you understand how to apply the computer to meet your own personal needs.

Type of software   Once you have acquired the necessary software, the first step in training to use the program consists mainly of reading the manual and following instructions. Generally, it is not necessary to understand the inner workings of a software program in order to use it, but you must understand all the functions and commands for a given program in order to utilize it most effectively.

Learning to use some particular software programs may be difficult because formal training is not as available for software use as it is for learning to operate the computers themselves. In order to locate formal training available in your area, scan announcements in the business section of your paper, contact vocational and technical schools, and make inquiries at computer/software stores.

In most cases, users of marketed software programs are self-taught. Finding needed information about a given program may be largely a matter of digging through computer magazines, books, and periodicals. While most computer magazines do carry helpful articles about particular programs, this is not a very dependable source of information; it is merely a matter of chance if your program is the topic of an article.

Very popular software packages are often the topics of books ranging from technical tutorials to simple how-to books. As another resource, nearly all large software companies provide technical support for their programs to consumers. Often this support is provided through a call-in phone line, giving you immediate answers to your problems. Computer user groups, mentioned earlier, and individuals who are familiar with a specific program are two other possible sources of help.

A word of caution is in order about the skills necessary to use software programs. Don't expect to be able to understand and use a program which performs a function you know nothing about. For example, if you don't know the first thing about accounting, it will be extremely difficult, if not impossible, for you to understand and operate most accounting software packages. A general rule of thumb is that you should have at least some knowledge of whatever functions your selected software performs.

For software used in conjunction with business microcomputer systems, which are not likely to be the type purchased by the home entrepreneur, training and technical support are often included as part of the computer package, as is the software itself. Training for use of business software packages may also be in-house, offered as part of your on-the-job training. In-house training may be in the form of small classes or one-to-one instruction from personnel experienced in using the program(s). In some cases, employees may be sent to computer companies for training seminars.

The increased use of computers among traditional businesses and industries has changed the complexion of our entire job market. It can also be said that, with the explosion of microcomputers on the market, home businesses are joining the computer age. And it seems evident that many people are eagerly and creatively developing electronic home enterprises to take advantage of this new technology.

Outlook on Opportunities

Unlike most other areas of employment, it is difficult to project figures for employment outlook and income levels within the realm of home businesses since there is such a diversity in all aspects of home enterprises. Occupations represented, amount of time and effort expended, levels of training or skills of entrepreneurs, previous business experience—all of these may vary tremendously, thus making meaningful statistics and predictions extremely difficult. Governmental and institutional studies of home businesses, discussed further in chapter 10, should supply a more factual information base for this growing sector of our economy.

A 1987 survey conducted by Sharp Electronics of 2,500 home professionals gives a profile of who is currently working from home. Contrary to popular images, male home workers outnumbered women, 60 percent to 40 percent. The average age of these home entrepreneurs was 46 years. Of all business owners, 85 percent were married, and at least one half of their spouses worked at least part time in the home business. The median income of those in the survey was $42,800,and 16 percent held a four-year college degree.

If you are interested in starting a particular kind of business, market research will help you ascertain whether there is sufficient demand for such a business. Those interested in a specific occupation will find that there are numerous career guidance books available which describe employment outlook as well as salary levels that can be expected. Much of the content of those books will hold true for home businesses in the same field.

The outlook for telecommuting stands out, however, since projections of its growth reflect more predictable interest from large companies that appear to be discovering the definite benefits this arrangement provides them. If we do indeed see the number of telecommuting positions increase to ten million in the next decade, as many experts are predicting, employment projections are quite bright for these types of positions.

Due to higher work efficiency, telecommuters doing various types of data processing generally earn more than their office counterparts. This is possible because these jobs are usually paid on a piecework basis. However, telecommuters may not receive the same fringe benefits as those data processors who work full-time in a traditional office position. If you are considering this type of work, be sure that you can afford to do without these benefits, if necessary.

Succeeding Financially

Anyone can start a home business, but not everyone will be able to make her or his business financially successful. If you look at figures based on small business start-ups, this becomes quite apparent. Of small businesses started in the United States in any given year, a full third will fail within three years. Within five years, over one half of the original number of businesses will fail. So, statistically speaking, chances of succeeding in a home business venture are about fifty-fifty. Of course, the better researched, financed, and planned your business is, the better are your chances of success.

A person working at home should expect to earn as much per hour as a person performing similar work in the traditional outside labor force. This would, of course, only hold true once your business has become established, since it normally takes months or even a year or so for most businesses to reach the break-even point. If you are unable to devote a great many hours to your business, your annual income will be understandably smaller when compared to the salary you would draw in similar, but traditional, full-time employment.

By being able to deduct the costs of materials and other overhead expenses from federal income taxes, home business owners can often keep more of their income. Conversely, an individual can expect to pay more for health and life insurance policies that are usually included in fringe benefit packages for traditional employees. Transportation expenses and a portion of rent or mortgage payments may also be deducted if part of the home is used as office space. Home-based workers also have less overhead than traditional businesses. It has been estimated that you can thus keep as much as fifteen percent more of your income by working at home as opposed to renting an office or other work space.

Life-style Choice

The decision to work at home must be based on more than monetary considerations. Working at home represents a drastic change in life-style from traditional employment, and this should be thoroughly contemplated by the would-be home worker.

For some people, no amount of money would be great enough to induce them to work at home. For others, the life-style changes resultant from working at home are nearly as valuable, and in some cases more valuable, than the money earned in the business.

Such decisions are extremely personal, so only you can determine whether a home business is the best work alternative for you. Being accurate in this assessment is probably the biggest factor in determining your own employment outlook in the home business field.

Assuring Business Success

Practically anyone can start a business. The key issue is whether or not you can make the business succeed, thereby keeping yourself employed and giving you a dependable income.

Most home businesses are largely reflections of the people who start and operate them, and many characteristics of the businesses can be attributed to the home-based entrepreneurs. What qualities do successful home enterprises have in common?

Fulfillment of market needs

More important than anything else, you must possess adequate knowledge of your potential market. To succeed, there must be a demand that your business fills. You have to recognize exactly what those needs are for your potential market. The more knowledgeable you are about your market, the better able you will be to take advantage of market needs.

Strong entrepreneurial skills

Nearly every business person feels that the willingness to take calculated risks is vital to running a successful business. These people possess strong decision-making capabilities and good leadership abilities. Further, beyond merely having good ideas, successful home business owners act on their ideas. They are doers as well as thinkers. In short, they have good entrepreneurial skills.

Utilization of special skills and knowledge

Smart business people make use of their areas of strength. They wisely select businesses that make use of their education, knowledge, and special skills. By working within your area of expertise and hiring professionals to perform tasks at which you are not particularly skilled, you can do much to assure the success of a business.

Working within the scope of your special knowledge need not drastically reduce your choice of businesses you might run. Many entrepreneurs have started successful businesses in areas that were somewhat related to their training and experience, not necessarily exactly in the area for which they were trained. For example, someone trained as a teacher might sell educational toys, open a day-care center, do free-lance writing, or start a business related to the subject matter taught, such as a history teacher guiding historical tours and tracing family genealogies. The point is to make good use of the skills and training you already have, rather than to start a business about which you know nothing.

Effective marketing strategies

In successful home business ventures, you will find that the business owners know how to market themselves and their products or services. Good marketing is just as important as a quality product or service because the public must perceive a product or service as worth purchasing before they will actually buy and try it.

Poor or nonexistent marketing will mean that consumers will not have a favorable impression of your business or even know what it has to offer. Good marketing, on the other hand, will make people feel good about your product or service and, more important, know that it is to their benefit to purchase and use it.

Sensitivity to market changes

Astute business people demonstrate flexibility in adjusting to market changes. Rather than stick stubbornly to a product or service that is obviously not doing well, wise business people read the changes in the market and either add new products or services or redevelop old ones to meet the new needs of their market.

Diversity in business

For many businesses, offering one product or service is just not profitable enough to make the business a going concern. Repeat business is more likely if you have more than one thing to offer your customers. You are also more likely to appeal to a wider range of customers if you have a broader spectrum of products or services.

On the other hand, home business owners should be cautious about overdiversifying their businesses. Offering too many products or services can contribute to overhead, make business operation complex, and dissipate efforts and energy.

Quality of products or services

In any market, people look for quality in a service or product. Businesses with products that are durable and well made or services that are well performed and dependable have a competitive edge over other firms. Quality assures customer satisfaction, and it will bring more business from repeat customers and clients who have had your firm recommended to them.

Willingness to work hard

Talk to any self-employed person and chances are that that person works sixty hours or more per week. Especially when starting businesses, home entrepreneurs find that they must devote a great many hours to getting their businesses off the ground—many more hours than one would work at traditional full-time jobs. Successful business owners are willing, and actually eager, to spend time working to begin, improve, and expand their businesses. These people enjoy the challenges and satisfaction their work brings them.

Sufficient start-up capital

Having sufficient start-up capital is essential to giving any business a good start. Different types of enterprises require different amounts of initial cash outlay, depending on the equipment, materials, and other expenses necessary to start in business. Consequently, what is a sufficient amount of capital for one business may not be nearly enough to start another.

A certain amount of scrimping during the initial stages of a business is probably wise. Careful use of money usually shows good business sense. Just be sure that you are not hobbling your business by starting with less money than you need.

Family cooperation

Home businesses, unlike traditional business ventures, require the support and cooperation of family members as well as that of employees and business associates. Many home businesses are also family businesses because the spouse and/or children in the family may also work in the venture, either as temporary help to get things started or as permanent employees or partners.

Whether or not family members work for the business, their support is crucial to its success. It is essential that family members respect the business part of the home, are courteous to customers, and answer the phone in a businesslike manner. Perhaps more important, a family's emotional support allows the home-based worker to place her or his full energies into running the business.

Pitfalls to Avoid

In addition to things you can do to assure success in your home business venture, there are also several things you should avoid. The following list of "Don'ts" may be just as valuable to follow as the things you should do.

- Don't fail to take your business seriously. Make sure you, your family, and friends treat your business as the professional endeavor it is.

- Don't fail to look for and heed professional advice. Be sure to consult with lawyers, accountants, insurance salespeople. You can also consult written sources of information.

- Don't neglect to register with the appropriate state and local authorities. Ignoring or making mistakes about tax and labor laws can cause you a lot of trouble.

- Don't forget to register with the state to get a state sales tax number. In addition to taking care of your taxes, this will allow you access to trade shows and wholesale discounts.

- Don't overlook or refuse back-up help. As soon as you can afford it, get the help you need in the areas of child care, housekeeping, and cooking, as well as for time-consuming routine business tasks.

- Don't fail to make use of labor-saving devices that are available to you.

- Don't confine testing of a product or idea to the workshop or drawing board. Find potential users, give them your products, and ask for their honest reactions.

- Don't study opportunity to death. When you get an idea, try it, fine-tune it, then do it.

Remember, when you start a business, you will probably face many obstacles, some that could put you under. Entrepreneurs seem to thrive on such challenges and are happy to live by their wits. To succeed against the big guy, you must play to your advantages: speed and flexibility. Adjust your course. Change tactics. It's better to make a wrong decision than none at all. Keep in mind that your own opportunity outlook is dependent on you.

Current Trends

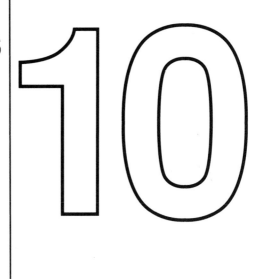

When Coralee Smith Kern started her cleaning service, Maid-to-Order, from her Chicago apartment in the early 1970s, serious business people just didn't run businesses from their homes. Those who did were often embarrassed by their home business status. Some people, Kern included, even went so far as to rent office space or a private post office box so as to have a "legitimate" business address.

Today, however, attitudes are changing about home businesses. As more home businesses appear, there is a growing awareness of cottage industries in the media, government, and the population at large. More and more people are recognizing the home not only as a legitimate place of business but as the best place for their particular business needs.

Changing Attitudes and Statistics

There are signs that many people are taking the idea of working from home seriously. Universities are studying home businesses; books are being written on the subject; and newspapers, magazines, and television are doing features about working from home. A growing number of companies are running experimental programs to see if telecommuting is a viable option for some of their workers. Even the government is looking at the possibility of having selected groups of government employees perform their work from home.

Recent changes in the American business climate are helping advance the move toward business decentralization, promoting the growth of the number of home businesses. Consider the following statistics regarding the current nature of jobs and job holders in our country:

- Manufacturing currently accounts for less than twenty-five percent of total employment in the United States.

- Service-oriented work now accounts for more than sixty percent of total employment.

- Approximately fifty to fifty-five percent of jobs today are information-related activities. This percentage is expected to increase.

- More than fifty percent of women are now in the labor force. Women also account for a major share of prospective new additions to the work force.

According to *Megatrends* author John Naisbett, beginning in 1986, when the last of the baby boom generation finished college and found employment, more people will leave the work force each year than join it. As a result, there will be labor shortages for the rest of the century.

As Naisbett sees it, corporations will have to change in order to compete for available workers. The result will be new models of employment including increases in part-time work, flexi-time, job sharing, flexi-place, and perhaps proportional benefits or even full benefits for part-time employees. Such steps in changing employment to suit workers' needs may become necessary in order for companies to compete for employees.

Statistics from the U.S. Chamber of Commerce indicate that as many as twenty-three million businesses filing tax returns list their home address as their place of business. This figure represents a fifty percent increase over that of a mere ten years ago. Nearly all available statistics on home business show continued growth in the work-at-home movement.

In large part, the increase in home businesses is due to the rapid proliferation of home computers. Recent research indicates that fifteen percent of households currently own computers. An additional six percent of households plan to purchase a personal computer within the next year. Clearly, microcomputers have the potential of being the single most influential factor in the work world as we know it.

Growing Trends

With such major changes in the world of work, we can expect to see dramatic reshaping of our conceptions about work in the next decade and beyond. What trends are apparent within the cottage industry?

Professionals working at home

Experts on the subject of home businesses expect that we will see a growth in the number of professional people who work at home. Lawyers, psychiatrists, and other professionals in greater number are beginning to use offices in their homes, and this trend is expected to continue.

Full-time home work

We can also expect to see more full-time home business people. At the present time, many home businesses provide supplementary income and are undertaken primarily as part-time ventures.

However, as home businesses become more widely accepted and already existing part-time ventures become more successful, we can expect to see many more full-time home businesses. Part of the reason for this is that, for the first time, many people are realizing that a home business can actually generate sufficient income on which to live.

Service businesses

Some studies have given us insight into the types of businesses being run from home. AT&T found that it is most common to provide a service. Since service businesses also represent the largest growth segment in traditional business, this trend will no doubt continue.

Growth in telecommuting

An estimated fifteen thousand people are telecommuting in the United States today. As pilot programs prove successful and more companies become involved, the number of telecommuters is expected to skyrocket.

The 1986 National Work-At-Home Survey found that about 11.4 percent of employed men work from home while 13.8 percent of employed women work from home. Of female home workers, 61.5 percent are self-employed while 38.5 percent are corporate employees. For males, 54.4 percent are self-employed; 45.5 percent are corporate employees. Many of those who are corporate employees engage in some form of telecommuting.

Jack Nilles, a director at the University of Southern California's Center for Future Research, predicts that by the early 1990s, ten million people will be telecommuting, at least part-time. The World Future Society, also projecting huge growth in this area, estimates that by the year 2000, a full third of the American work force will be telecommuting.

The trend will be for more and more telecommunication by the end of this century. The increased affordability of personal computers will also open opportunities for home businesses, such as word processing, which heretofore were not practical to operate from the home.

The microcomputer industry itself is an outgrowth of the work-at-home movement. Steven Jobs and Steven Wozniak designed what was to become the Apple I computer in Wozniak's apartment and built the first Apples in Jobs's garage. It's also interesting to note that about sixty percent of the current microcomputer software industry is home based.

Increasing government interest

Government has taken a more active interest in home-based business as evidenced by recent activities. In 1983 the Senate held hearings on cottage industries, and several branches of the federal government have funded research projects to study different aspects of home-based businesses.

The U.S. Small Business Administration funded a study in 1985 to do the following:

- Research the information currently available on home businesses.

- Develop a questionnaire to find out the number and some of the demographics of home businesses in the country.

- Determine the best avenue of administering such a survey so as to be most representative of the population of the United States as a whole.

Various governmental, educational, and business organizations are carrying out a variety of studies on home business. All have much to gain by gathering and studying specific statistics and other information related to cottage industries. This surge of interest follows a number of years of home businesses being virtually ignored by the government and other research bodies.

Growth of professional associations and publications

Professional and trade associations are springing up across the country in response to the rapid growth in the number of home business entrepreneurs. (The Appendix contains names and addresses of many pertinent professional and trade groups.)

To supply home workers with up-to-date business information, several of these associations publish newsletters that also keep members informed of new developments in the home business world. A few associations also provide insurance and discount benefits that are not otherwise readily available to the self-employed home business person.

The most important role of these associations, however, may be in serving as advocates representing the unique interests of the home worker. By serving as clearinghouses of home business information and by working to influence legislation, these professional associations seek to help protect the rights of all people to choose their workplace, whether that be in the home or in a traditional business setting.

Expansion of training opportunities

Numerous individuals, groups, organizations, and institutions have developed a wide range of training opportunities to meet the needs of home workers. These range from general workshops on starting a home-based business to very specific, single-topic seminars.

Special seminars may cover a topic of general concern, such as those offered on bookkeeping, legal issues, or tax deductions for home businesses. Others, for a narrower audience, provide pointers on such things as running a particular type of home business. It's important that you seek out the specific kind of training you need.

Every home business person needs a substantial base of general business knowledge, and the most successful people are usually the ones who seek to keep their skills and knowledge current. Fortunately, this is becoming easier as the number and quality of training opportunities expand.

Recognizing the importance of small business in our economy and realizing the vital role that knowledge plays in successful business, a number of government and private agencies and organizations offer both educational opportunities and, in some cases, one-on-one informational assistance to home business owners. The Small Business Administration, S.C.O.R.E. (Service Corps of Retired Executives), and University Small Business Development Centers are just a few of the agencies currently offering these kinds of assistance.

Issues Affecting Home Businesses

As the number of people who work from home continues to increase, pressures are being exerted for and against altering laws and regulations affecting cottage industries. For people working from home, the major issues of the next decade will very likely be zoning, labor laws, and licensing.

Zoning laws

In the past, many ordinances were written to discourage home businesses for various reasons. These ordinances, which include outmoded zoning laws in many cities, make working at home legally a difficult proposition for some home entrepreneurs.

Since many municipalities have zoning laws that restrict home business, it is important to check your zoning laws before you start working at home or if you already have a business and don't know the specifics of your local ordinance. Once you are doing business in your home, zoning officers can shut down your operation, and many municipalities post a heavy per day fine if you continue to work after receiving a cease-and-desist notice.

When checking your local regulations, realize also that most zoning laws are written by *inclusion* rather than *exclusion,* which means that unless a type of business is specifically mentioned in an ordinance, it is not legal. This is especially problematic for computer-based businesses since many city zoning ordinances were written long before microcomputers became prevalent.

While some of these laws were sound at the time they were written, officials could not envision the revolutionary changes brought about by microcomputers and other technological advances. The following true story illustrates the problems that home businesses can have with zoning laws in their communities.

In August of 1983, a city inspector informed a Chicago couple that the city had received a complaint that they were violating the zoning laws by conducting a commercial enterprise in a residential area. Two days later, upon receipt of official notice that their use of computer equipment in the home was indeed illegal, they read the part of the zoning ordinance that applied to their home computer. They were shocked to find that it said the following:

> Home occupation. A physician, dentist, lawyer, clergyman or other professional person may use his residence for consultation, emergency treatment or performance of religious rites, but not for the general practice of his profession and not for the installation or use of any mechanical or electrical equipment customarily incident to the practice of such profession.

Many home-based business people either don't know, or don't really want to know, the specifics of their local zoning laws. "If they don't bother me, I won't bother them," is an easy position to take.

One pays a price for doing so, however. It's hard to concentrate fully on your work when energies are dissipated in wondering if someone will "blow the whistle" on you. It's even more disturbing to use precious time that should be spent on your work "fighting city hall."

Of course, none of us wants a home business next door disrupting our home life. Reasonable guidelines should be established to guard neighborhoods from businesses that create undue noise or traffic or pose a threat to safety. Electronic cottages in particular, and the majority of other cottage industries as well, are clean, safe, and low profile. In fact, often neighbors don't even know they are there.

There is evidence that the status of the zoning issue is already beginning to change. Organizations for home business people are working to help city governments write zoning laws that allow home businesses to operate while at the same time protect the rights of local residential citizens.

In order to help home workers battle outmoded zoning regulations, several organizations have written model zoning ordinances. These model ordinances, intended to protect both the home business and the residential neighborhood, have been developed to serve as examples for cities nationwide wishing to update their zoning laws.

If your local zoning laws prohibit or severely restrict home businesses, you may want to band together with other like-minded citizens in your area and approach your city council about having the ordinance changed to reflect current community needs. Changes in the world of work have resulted in a period of cultural lag, producing confusion and problems, but our laws are bound to catch up quickly with the new age of technology.

Labor laws   In addition to problems with local zoning ordinances, home business people need to be concerned about legislation on the state and federal levels. This is true even though many home workers do not realize the potential effects that such legislation may have on them.

The worksteaders' right to work at home continues to be challenged in many states with laws and/or amendments to the long-standing Industrial Home Work Act of 1943. Basically, the Industrial Home Work Act originally banned seven areas of home work, specifically the manufacture of gloves and mittens, knitted outerwear, embroideries, buttons and buckles, handkerchiefs, jewelry, and women's apparel.

Knitted outerwear, which was originally included in the ban, was the subject of great controversy and even litigation several years ago. As a result, the government lifted the ban only on knitted outerwear, which could then be made legally in the home. Production of the other items continued to be illegal as home occupations.

In 1984, Bill S665, or the "Freedom of the Workplace Act, V," was introduced in the U.S. Senate in response to the issue of home production of knitted outerwear and the decision of the Appeals Court on the matter. In effect, this bill proposed to lift the bans on all classifications of home work prohibited by the Industrial Home Work Act of 1943 and allow home work for any occupation without requiring special permits. The intention of the bill was to allow any person—but particularly mothers of small children, retirees, disabled individuals, and other people with limited mobility—to work at home without the restraints imposed by the Fair Labor Standards Act of 1938 and the Industrial Home Work Act of 1943.

The U.S. Chamber of Commerce strongly supported this legislation because they believed that it fostered freedom to work and would help to prevent labor monopolies. Although the bill was never passed, on November 11, 1988, the Labor Department announced that it would lift the ban on industrial home work in all industries except women's apparel. The other requirements and protections outlined by the Fair Labor Standards Act would remain in effect, including the guarantees of minimum wage and overtime protections. This ruling went into effect as of January 9, 1989. This decision has the potential of making home work a viable option for thousands of Americans skilled in these seven traditional crafts. However, in response to this ruling, apparel unions have raised suit in the U.S. District Court to keep the ban intact. At this point, the outcome of the case is uncertain.

While unions are not primarily concerned with the self-employed person, some home-based workers fear that the scope of these laws and regulations could be extended eventually to create a blockade to all home-based service and product businesses, including electronic cottages.

Feeling that cottage industries threaten the job security of their members and that some cottage industry workers may be exploited, several unions are applying pressure on Congress and several state legislative bodies to limit or ban additional areas of home work.

While the majority of unions are primarily concerned with industrial home work, a segment of organized labor is opposed to all types of piecework being performed in the home—including most work that falls into the category of telecommuting. Fearing the development of what is being termed the electronic sweatshop, many union officials claim that allowing telecommuting to go on opens the door for worker exploitation.

In October of 1983, the AFL-CIO passed a resolution calling for a ban on computer home work, except in the case of the handicapped. The Service Employees International Union prohibits its membership, which includes clerical workers and data processors, from telecommuting.

The AFL-CIO, afraid of losing members or being unable to organize workers if they are dispersed in homes, called for expanding the current prohibitions to include computer terminal work in 1987. Under the proposed certification system, companies could employ home workers by getting a government certificate.

While there are no current state or federal laws specifically outlawing home computer businesses, several states do have laws, depending on their interpretation and enforcement, that could pose a threat to computer home workers.

On the other side of the issue, another professional group, the Association of Electronic Cottagers (AEC), has set out to protect the rights of its members who represent the growing number of people who work in their homes with personal computers. Group membership includes providers of computer services, telecommuters, and home businesses using computers.

The AEC has authored "The Electronic Cottage Bill of Rights" whose first provision summarizes the sentiments of home worker groups in general: "Legislatures shall make no laws prohibiting freedom of opportunity to work in one's home with a computing and/or robotic device when that work does not interfere with neighbors' enjoyment of their own homes and communities."

Supporters of the right to work at home point out that most people who work at home choose to do so because, for them, the rewards are greater. Telecommuting and working at home in general should remain voluntary, they maintain. While labor unions are generally opposed to home work, it may well be their own rank and file who, having tried and liked home work, sway the opinions of the unions. Or it may be that the size and momentum of the work-at-home movement will cause legislators to side with those who advocate the right to choose one's work place.

Since national and state labor laws and local zoning ordinances must be obeyed, home business owners as individuals and in professional groups must, of necessity, keep careful watch over what is and will be happening in our legislative bodies over the next few years.

Licensing As problems with zoning and labor laws and their detrimental effects on home business are resolved, the licensing of home businesses may become a bigger concern than ever.

With traditional businesses it is fairly easy for various levels of government to keep track of the existence of a business, its earnings, and other information of concern to the government. The presence of a traditional business in a community is readily apparent. It is usually located in a commercial building in a business district; it is open to the public; and, given financial restraints, it is widely advertised. The business name is often in the phone directory and its mailing address normally refers to the business by name.

None of the points which make a traditional business easily visible to the government are necessarily true of a home business. Home businesses are located in people's homes, usually in residential areas. A great many home businesses are low-profile with regard to advertising and public access. And while the name of a home business may be listed in the telephone book and used as part of a mailing address, just as often it is not.

It is precisely because of this low-profile image of home businesses that the government is concerned with the licensing of home-based businesses. At present, all businesses must be registered with the federal government so that they can be issued a tax identification number and, ostensibly, pay taxes on their earnings. Some government officials feel that it would be too easy for unscrupulous home business people to not register their businesses and thus avoid paying taxes on their earnings.

At this point the topic is largely speculative, but licenses for home businesses are likely to comprise a special category. Further, applicants may have to meet restrictions or special requirements in order to be allowed a license to operate their businesses. While licensing in some states and locales is already required, we can expect to see more widespread licensing requirements for home businesses and perhaps even federal licensing and regulation of home businesses and home business standards.

Government's role
Government may serve as a positive influence in the growth of cottage industries if the legislative and regulatory climate continues to be supportive of small business and if the government is responsive to the needs of its home business constituency. As more and more people work from home, government support of this work alternative will undoubtedly grow stronger.

But while we are in a period of change, confusion often exists. Governmental groups, for example, are occasionally found to be working against one another on the problems surrounding home work.

Labor regulations provide an example of this lack of consistency. While state and local laws often prevent working at home, many state agencies—including those in Oregon, Kentucky, Minnesota, South Carolina, North Carolina, Virginia, and West Virginia—have offered support of efforts to permit freedom to work at home. Many of these agencies offer assistance in the form of seminars, workshops, and individual consulting sessions to aid people in setting up home businesses.

Many of these efforts are supported, either directly or indirectly, through government funding. Government agencies, of course, are funded directly by the government; but other privately directed assistance to home businesses is sometimes also funded indirectly through government grants. For example, the American Woman's Economic Development Center was formed with a federal grant. Funded by both the government and the private sector, this organization helps women to start businesses, whether in their homes or elsewhere, by offering educational seminars, management training, and technical assistance.

Preparing for Change

In light of the issues connected with home business and the rapidly changing world of work, particularly in the home business sector, how can you, as a potential home business person, best prepare for the changes that may occur?

Learn all you can. One of the best ways to prepare for change is to make the most of opportunities to gather knowledge and develop skills. If you are deciding on a career, study topics that interest you and are related to your possible career choices.

The specific information that you study is not always the crucial aspect of this learning process. What you learn now may have applications at some point in your future, although they are not apparent at the present. More important, learn to learn so that you will be able to take advantage of changes and have the resources to deal with them as they occur throughout your life.

Education is an ongoing process, and reading is one of the most enriching avenues to gaining knowledge. If you are interested in pursuing a home business career, read pertinent career guidance books, books on business and home business, and information on the particular fields that interest you.

Actual work experience will also enhance your chance of life-long success in the world of work. Learning by doing adds an important dimension to your learning experiences.

Anticipate change. Very few things stay the same. This seems to be especially true about our economy, the job market, and the world of work. By making a conscious effort to anticipate changes in these areas, you can better prepare yourself for an occupation that will be in demand. Make note of newspaper articles about growth projections for various careers. Seek out information that will help you ascertain the shifting demands of our society in the immediate future.

It is interesting to note that experts on the subject of careers are now saying that working people, on the average, will shift careers every five to ten years. This means that the average worker can expect to have a minimum of four different careers before retirement. Regardless of the career you initially select, be flexible and prepare for these possible occupational changes.

Keep informed. Particularly in light of all the issues which could affect home businesses, it is important to keep informed. Read newspapers and news magazines; watch or listen to the news; and keep abreast of what is happening, especially regarding legislation that affects business and home business in particular. Business news and news about technological advances and other topics affecting the work world should also be of interest to the home business owner.

Take an active stance. To a certain extent, everyone can have an effect on the changes that do occur. If you feel strongly about an issue, such as legislation affecting your business, take an active stance on the matter. You can write letters, inform others about the possible effects of the change, or join an association of people with common concerns. You can influence change, but only if you actively try to do so.

Work to achieve your goals. We all have dreams and aspirations. The people who achieve their dreams are most often those who set goals and then work to attain them. Home business entrepreneurs are doers as well as dreamers. If you want a home-based occupation, or anything else for that matter, be persistent yet flexible. Learn to take advantage of change. Many entrepreneurs have found their greatest opportunities in times of change and even adversity. With faith in yourself and plenty of hard work, you can make your dreams a reality.

Appendix:
Sources of
Additional
Information

Books

Anatomy of a Business Plan. Linda Pinson and Jerry Jennett. Fullerton, Calif.: Out of Your Mind . . . and Into the Marketplace, 1988.

How to Borrow Money from a Bank. Don H. Alexander. New York: Beaufort Books, 1984.

Basic Accounting for the Small Business. Clive G. Cornish. Seattle: Self-Counsel Press, Inc., 1984.

Becoming Self-Employed: First Hand Advice from Those Who Have Done It. Susan Elliott. Blue Ridge, Penn.: Liberty (a division of TAB Books), 1987.

The Business Planning Guide: Creating a Plan for Success in Your Own Business. David H. Bangs, Jr. Dover, N.H.: Upstart Publishing Company, 1988.

The Complete No Nonsense Success Library. Steve Kahn. Stamford, Conn.: Longmeadow Press.

Complete Start-Up Kit for a Business with Your Computer. Paul and Sarah Edwards. Santa Monica, Calif.: Here's How, 1989.

Consultant's Kit: Establishing and Operating Your Successful Consulting Business. Jeffrey L. Lant. Cambridge, Mass.: Jeffrey Lant Associates, 1981.

Developing Target Markets. John H. Melchinger. Southborough, Mass.: Educational Training Systems, Inc.

Directory of Online Databases. Santa Monica, Calif.: Caudra Associates, Inc. (Published quarterly.)

Do What You Love—The Money Will Follow. Marsha Sinetar. New York: Paulist Press, 1987.

Entrepreneurial Mothers. Phyllis Gillis. New York: Rawson Associates, 1984.

Entrepreneurial Women. Colleen Perri. Kenosha, Wis.: Possibilities Publishing, 1987.

The Entrepreneur's Complete Self-Assessment Guide. Douglas A. Gray. Seattle: Self-Counsel Press Inc., 1986.

Freelance Food-Crafting. Janet Shown. Boulder, Colo.: Live Oak Publications, 1983.

Freelance Forever: Successful Self-Employment. Marietta Whittlesey. New York: Avon, 1982.

Growing a Business—Raising a Family: Ideas and Inspiration for the Work-at-Home Parent. Jan Fletcher and Charlie Fletcher, eds. Seattle: NextStep Publications, 1988.

A Guide to Fairs and Festivals in the United States. Frances Shemanski. Westport, Conn.: Greenwood Press, 1984.

Help for Your Growing Home-Based Business. Barbara Brabec. Naperville, Ill.: Brabec Productions.

Homemade Money: The Definitive Guide to Success in a Home Business. Barbara Brabec. White Hall, Va.: Betterway Publications, 1984.

Honest Business: A Superb Strategy for Starting and Managing Your Own Business. Michael Phillips and Salli Rasberry. New York: Random House, 1981.

How to Cash in on Your Bright Ideas. George G. Siposs. Costa Mesa, Calif.: Universal Developments.

How to Earn $15 to $50 an Hour and More with a Pickup Truck or Van. Don Lilly. Phoenix: Darien Books, 1983.

How to Finance Your Small Business with Government Money: SBA Loans. Rick Stephan Hayes. New York: Wiley, 1983.

How to Form Your Own Corporation without a Lawyer for Under $50.00. Ted Nicholas. Wilmington, Del.: Enterprise Publishing, Inc., 1981.

How to Make Big Money at Home. Ronald J. Cooke. Montreal: Eden Press, 1986.

How to Make Newsletters, Brochures and Other Good Stuff without a Computer System. H. Gregory. Sedro-Woolley, Wash.: Pinstripe Publishing, 1985.

How to Open and Operate a Bed and Breakfast Home. Jan Stankus. Chester, Conn.: The Globe Pequot Press, 1986.

How to Open (and Successfully Operate) a Country Inn: Guest Houses, Bed and Breakfast Homes, Small Hotels, Lodges. Karen L. Estsell with Elaine C. Brennan. Stockbridge, Mass.: The Bershire Traveller Press, Inc., 1983.

How to Prosper in Your Own Business—Getting Started and Staying on Course. Brian R. Smith. Brattleboro, Vt.: The Stephen Green Press, 1981.

How to Run a Small Business. J. K. Lasser, ed. Manchester, Mo.: McGraw-Hill Book Company, 1988.

How to Start a Profitable Child Care Program in Your Home. Patricia Gallagher. Worcester, Penn.: Child Care and You.

How to Start a Successful Word Processing Business in Your Home. Penny McBride, P.O. Box 2133, Leucadia, CA 92024.

How to Start Your Own Bed and Breakfast: A Guide to Hosting Paying Guests in Your House or Apartment. Mary Zander. Spencertown, N.Y.: Golden Hill Press, 1985.

Idea to Marketplace: An Inventor's Guide. Thomas R. Lampe. Los Angeles: Price Stern Sloan, 1988.

Ideas That Work: Ten of Today's Most Exciting and Profitable Self-Employment Opportunities. Susan Elliott. Boulder, Colo.: Live Oak Publications, 1985.

Information Payoff: The Transformation of Work in the Electronic Age. Paul A. Strassman. New York: The Free Press, 1985.

Inside the Family Business. Leon Danco. Cleveland, Ohio: University Press, 1980.

I've Got a Great Idea. Scotty Williams, P.O. Box 927, Abilene, TX 79604.

Jobs: How People Create Their Own. William C. Ronco. Boston: Beacon Press, 1977.

Ladybucks. Valerie Bohigian. New York: Dodd, Mead.

The Loan Package. Emmett Ramey and Alex Wong. Sunnyvale, Calif.: Successful Business Library, 1982.

Managing the One-Person Business. Mary Jean Parson. New York: Dodd, Mead, 1987.

Marketing: Researching and Reaching Your Target Market. Linda Pinson and Jerry Jennett. Fullerton, Calif.: Out of Your Mind . . . and Into the Marketplace, 1988.

Marketing without Advertising. Michael Phillips and Salli Rasberry. Laytonville, Calif.: In Business Bookshelf, 1986.

Marketing Your Product. Douglas A. Gray and Donald Cyr. Seattle: Self-Counsel Press Inc., 1987.

Marketing Your Service. Jean Withers and Carol Vipperman. Seattle: Self-Counsel Press Inc., 1987.

Megatrends: Ten New Directions Transforming Our Lives. John Naisbitt. New York: Warner Books, Inc.: 1982.

Mothering and Managing a Mail-Order Business at Home. MHBN, P.O. Box 423, East Meadow, NY 11554.

Mothering and Managing a Typing Service at Home. MHBN, P.O. Box 423, East Meadow, NY 11554.

The New Entrepreneurs: Women Working from Home. Terri and Nona Tepper. New York: Universe Books, 1980.

Office at Home. Robert Scott. New York: Scribner's, 1985.

Out of Your Mind—and Into the Marketplace. Linda Pinson and Jerry Jennett. Fullerton, Calif.: Out of Your Mind . . . and Into the Marketplace, 1988.

Out on Your Own: From Corporate to Self-Employment. Robert W. Bly and Gary Blake. New York: John Wiley and Sons, 1986.

The Partnership Book. Denis Clifford and Ralph Warner. Berkeley, Calif.: Nolo Press, 1987.

Real Money from Home: How to Start, Manage, and Profit from a Home-Based Service Business. Valerie Bohigian. New York: New American Library, 1985.

Selling Ideas. Chase Revel and Don Kracke. Los Angeles: American Entrepreneurs Association, 1980.

Small Business Works—How to Operate and Win in the Free Enterprise System. Eugene L. Gross, et. al. New York: AMACOM, 1977.

Small Time Operator. Bernard Kamoroff. Laytonville, Calif.: Bell Springs Publishers, 1986.

So You've Got a Great Idea. Steve Fiffer. Reading, Mass.: Addison-Wesley, 1986.

So You Want to Be Your Own Boss: Women's Guide to Opening a Small Business. Susan Milby. Florida Economic Development Center, 325 College of Business, Florida State University, Tallahassee, FL 32306-1007.

Start and Run a Profitable Craft Business. William G. Hynes. Seattle: Self-Counsel Press Inc., 1986.

Start and Run a Profitable Consulting Business. Douglas A. Gray. Seattle: Self-Counsel Press Inc., 1986.

Start and Run a Profitable Restaurant. Michael M. Coltman. Seattle: Self-Counsel Press Inc., 1983.

Start and Run a Profitable Retail Business. Michael M. Coltman. Seattle: Self-Counsel Press Inc., 1983.

Starting a Home Based Business. Frederick H. Rice. Winoski, Vt.: University of Vermont Extension Service, 1985.

Starting a Mini-Business: A Guidebook for Seniors. Nancy Olson. Sunnyvale, Calif.: Fair Oaks Publishing Company, 1988.

Starting on a Shoestring. Arnold S. Goldstein. New York: Wiley, 1988.

Telecommuting: How to Make It Work for You and Your Company. Gil E. Gordon and Marcia Kelly. Englewood Cliffs, N.J.: Prentice-Hall, 1976.

That's a Great Idea! The New Product Handbook. Tony Husch and Linda Foust. Oakland, Calif.: Gravity Publishing, 1986.

The Third Wave. Alvin Toffler. New York: William Morrow and Company, 1980.

The Unabashed Self-Promoter's Guide: What Every Man, Woman, Child and Organization in America Needs to Know About Getting Ahead by Exploiting the Media. Jeffrey L. Lant. Cambridge, Mass.: Jeffrey Lant Associates, 1983.

We Own It: Starting and Managing Co-ops, Collectives and Employee Owned Ventures. Peter Honigsberg, et. al. Laytonville, Calif.: Bell Springs Publishers, 1982.

Word Processing Profits at Home. Peggy Glenn. Huntington Beach, Calif.: Aames-Allen Publishing, 1983.

The Work-at-Home Sourcebook. Lynie Arden. Boulder, Colo.: Live Oak Publications, 1987.

Working for Yourself: A Guide to Success for People Who Work Outside the 9 to 5 World. Phillip Namanworth and Gene Busnar. New York: McGraw-Hill, 1985.

Working from Home. Paul and Sarah Edwards. Los Angeles: Jeremy P. Tarcher, Inc., 1985.

Periodicals

Business Week
1221 Avenue of the Americas
New York, NY 10020
or
P.O. Box 430
Highstown, NJ 08520

Entrepreneur
2311 Pontius Avenue
Los Angeles, CA 90064

Fortune
1271 Avenue of the Americas
New York, NY 10020

The Futurist
The World Future Society
4916 St. Elmo Avenue
Bethesda, MD 20814

Harvard Business Review
P.O. Box 3000
Woburn, MA 01888

In Business
Box 351
Emmaus, PA 18049

INC.
36 Commercial Wharf Road
Boston, MA 02166

Info World
375 Cochituate Road
Framingham, MA 01701

Modern Office Procedures
1111 Chester Avenue
Cleveland, OH 44114

Mother Earth News
P.O. Box 70
Hendersonville, NC 28739

Mothering
P.O. Box 1690
Santa Fe, NM 87504

Nation's Business
4940 Nicholson Court
Kensington, MD 20895

Newsweek
444 Madison Avenue
New York, NY 10022

The Office
1200 Summer Street
Stamford, CT 06904

Savvy
P.O. Box 2495
Boulder, CO 80322

Success
P.O. Box 33000
Bergenfield, NH 07621

Technology Review
MIT
Room 10-140
Cambridge, MA 02139

U.S. News and World Report
2300 N Street, N.W.
Washington, DC 20037

Venture
P.O. Box 3206
Harlan, IA 51537

Working Woman
342 Madison Avenue
New York, NY 10017
or
P.O. Box 10130
Des Moines, IA 50349

Newsletters   *Challenges*
P.O. Box 22432
Kansas City, MO 64113-2432
(816) 363-6544
7 times per year

Direct Response Specialist
   P.O. Box 1075
   Tarpon Springs, FL 34286
   (813) 937-3480
   Monthly

Family Business Review
   Family Firm Institute
   P.O. Box 476
   Johnstown, NY 12095
   (518) 762-2853
   Bimonthly

Freelance Journal
   7507 Sunset Boulevard
   Suite 213
   Los Angeles, CA 90046
   (213) 874-8281
   Bimonthly

Home Business Advisor
   NextStep Publications
   P.O. Box 41108
   Fayetteville, NC 28309
   (919) 867-2128
   8 times per year

Home Business Advocate
   Wendy Priesnitz and Associates
   195 Markville Road
   Unionville, Ontario
   Canada L3R4V8

Home Business Line
   397 Post Road
   Darien, CT 06820
   (203) 655-4380
   Monthly

Home Business Monthly
   38 Briarcliffe Road
   Rochester, NY 14617
   (716) 338-1144
   Bimonthly

Home Enterprise Review
Sharon Robinson
P.O. Box 94028
Washington, MI 48084
(313) 254-3174
Quarterly

The Front Room News
P.O. Box 1541
Clifton, NJ 07015-1541
Bimonthly

Home-Work
P.O. Box 9825
College Station, TX 77840
(409) 693-4753
Monthly

Homeworking Mothers
P.O. Box 423
East Meadow, NY 11554
(516) 997-7394
Quarterly

Independent Publishers Trade Report
Greenfield Press
P.O. Box 176
Southport, CT 06490
(203) 268-4878
Monthly

Keyboard Connection
P.O. Box 338
Glen Carbon, IL 62034
Bimonthly

Long Island Freelance Network
(a division of the National Freelance Network)
415 Rutgers Road
West Babylon, NY 11704
(516) 422-9010
Bimonthly

Minding Your Own Business
John H. Melchinger Company
15 Cypress Street
Suite 207
Newton Centre, MA 02159-2231
(617) 969-0823
Bimonthly

National Home Business Report
    Barbara Brabeck Productions
    P.O. Box 2137
    Naperville, IL 60566
    (312) 971-1121
    Bimonthly

National Home-Work News
    933 N. Harrston Road
    Suite 7-136
    Stone Mountain, GA 30083
    (404) 498-2945
    Quarterly

The Newsletter
    League of N.H. Craftsmen
    205 N. Main Street
    Concord, NH 03301
    Bimonthly

The Professional Quilter
    Oliver Press Publications for Quilters
    Jeannie M. Spears, Editor
    Box 75277
    St. Paul, MN 55175-0277
    (612) 426-9681
    Quarterly

Sharing Ideas
    (Speakers Newsletter)
    Dottie Walters
    P.O. Box 1120
    18825 Hilcrest Road
    Glendora, CA 91740
    (818) 335-8069
    Bimonthly

Southwest Freelancer
    Deborah Robinson, Editor
    P.O. Box 160
    Morrow, AR 72749

Telecommuting Report
    Electronic Services Unlimited, Inc.
    142 W. 24th Street
    New York, NY 10011
    (516) 791-2332
    Monthly

Telecommuting Review, The Gordon Report
Telespan Publishing Corp.
50 W. Palm Street
Altadena, CA 91001
(818) 797-5482
Monthly

Woman's Workshop
(a national news journal for at-home moms)
Deborah L. Dawson
Christine S. Donovan
P.O. Box 843
Coronado, CA 92118
(619) 437-1350
Quarterly

Women & Co.
Bantam Doubleday Dell Publishing Group, Inc.
666 Fifth Avenue
35th Floor
New York, NY 10103
(212) 554-9614
Monthly

Worksteader News
TWN Publications
P.O. Box 820
Rancho Cordova, CA 95741
(916) 635-8764
Bimonthly

Audio/Video   *Be Your Own Boss. Sylvia Porter's Personal Finance Magazine,* New York, NY. One-hour cassette audio tape.

Effective Marketing for Service Businesses and Professional Practices. The Entrepreneur's Information Center, Boulder, Colorado. Two-hour cassette audio tape set.

The Entrepreneur Digest. Bill Bailey Communications, Inc. Two-hour cassette audio tape set.

How to Buy a Franchise. Wiley Sound Business Cassettebooks, New York, NY. Two-hour cassette audio tape set.

How to Get a Job Working from Home: Telecommuting and Other Options. Gil Gordon. Here's How, 2607 Second Street, Suite 3, Santa Monica, CA 90405. Two audio cassette tapes.

How to Make Money Doing Research with Your Computer. Sue Rugge. Here's How, 2607 Second Street, Suite 3, Santa Monica, CA 90405. Two audio cassette tapes.

How to Operate a Word Processing Service. Barbara Elman. Here's How, 2607 Second Street, Suite 3, Santa Monica, CA 90405. Two audio cassette tapes.

How to Profitably Sell the Software You Write: Writing, Publishing and Selling Software. Doug Carlston. Here's How, 2607 Second Street, Suite 3, Santa Monica, CA 90405. Two audio cassette tapes.

How to Publish a Profitable Newsletter: The Reasons and a Roadmap for Getting into Newsletter Publishing with Your Computer. J. Norman Goode. Here's How, 2607 Second Street, Suite 3, Santa Monica, CA 90405. Two audio cassette tapes.

How to Really Start Your Own Business. Inc. Publishing Corp., Ninety-minute video.

How to Start a Cleaning and Janitorial Service. Lynn Frances. Here's How, 2607 Second Street, Suite 3, Santa Monica, CA 90405.

How to Start and Manage a Computer Consulting Practice. William Slavin. Here's How, 2607 Second Street, Suite 3, Santa Monica, CA 90405. Two audio cassette tapes.

How to Succeed in a Home Business. Inc. Videos, P.O. Box 68618, 63601 LaPas Trail, Indianapolis, IN 46268-0618. One-hour video cassette.

Secrets to Success for Woman Entrepreneurs. The Entrepreneur's Information Center, Boulder, Colorado. Two-hour cassette audio tape set.

The Woman Entrepreneur: Do You Have What It Takes? United Home Video. Fifty-five-minute video.

Working from Home. Paul and Sarah Edwards. McGraw-Hill, Fullerton, CA 92631. Audio cassette.

Organizations and Associations

American Association of Professional Consultants
9140 Ward Parkway
Kansas City, MO 64114
(603) 623-5378

American Federation of Small Businesses
407 S. Dearborn Street
Chicago, IL 60608
(312) 427-0207

American Home Business Association
397 Post Road
Darien, CT 06820
(203) 655-4380/1-800-433-6361

American Home Sewing Association
1375 Broadway
4th Floor
New York, NY 10018
(212) 302-2150

The American Society of Interior Designers
1430 Broadway
New York, NY 10018
(212) 944-9220

Association of Desk-Top Publishers (AD-TP)
Box 881667
San Diego, CA 92108-0034

Association of Electronic Cottagers
(accessible online through the Working from Home
Forum)
CompuServe Information Service
5000 Arlington Centre Boulevard
Columbus, OH 45220
(800) 898-8990

Charted Designers of America, Inc.
P.O. Box 348
Elmwood Park, NJ 07407
(201) 794-1133/(201) 797-0657

Family Firm Institute
P.O. Box 476
Johnstown, NY 12095
(518) 762-3853

International Association of Independent Publishers
(COSMEP)
P.O. Box 703
San Francisco, CA 94101
(415) 922-9490

International Information/Word Processing Association
1015 N. York Road
Willow Grove, PA 19090
(215) 657-6300

Mothers Home Business Network (MHBN)
  P.O. Box 423
  East Meadow, NY 11554
  (516) 997-7394

National Association for the Cottage Industry
  P.O. Box 14460
  Chicago, IL 60614
  (312) 472-8116

National Association of Desktop Publishers (NADTP)
  P.O. Box 508
  Kenmore Station
  Boston, MA 02215
  (617) 437-6472

National Association of Entrepreneurial Couples
  P.O. Box 700
  Aptos, CA 95001-0700

National Association for the Self-Employed
  2324 Gravel Road
  Ft. Worth, TX 76118
  (817) 589-2475

National Association of Women Business Owners
  600 S. Federal Street
  Suite 400
  Chicago, IL 60605
  (312) 922-2734

National Computer Graphics Association
  2722 Merilee Drive
  Suite 200
  Fairfax, VA 22031
  (703) 698-9600

Newsletter Association
  1401 Wilson Boulevard
  Suite 403
  Arlington, VA 22209
  (703) 527-2333

Support Services Alliance
  P.O. Box 130
  Schocharie, NY 12157
  (212) 398-7800

Miscellaneous Resources

Achieving Success in Small Business. Minnesota Curriculum Services Center, 3554 White Bear Avenue, White Bear Lake, MN 55110. Notebook and accompanying audio tapes.

The Business Plan for Home-Based Business. SBA no. MA 2.028.

Business Planning Guide. Dottie Roberts. 1984. Florida Economic Development Center, 325 College of Business, Florida State University, Tallahassee, FL 32306-1007.

Business Use of Your Home. Pamphlet no. 587. U.S. Department of the Treasury, Internal Revenue Service, Central Area Distribution Center, 2402 E. Empire, Bloomington, IL 61704.

Catalog Directory. Roger Davis, Fax Marketing, 460 Carrollton Drive, Frederick, MD 21701. (301) 695-7018. Directory of over a thousand free catalogs.

Employers' Tax Guide—Circular E. Pamphlet no. 15. U.S. Department of the Treasury, Internal Revenue Service, Central Area Distribution Center, 2402 E. Empire, Bloomington, IL 61704.

The Entrepreneur Kit. Grand Forks, ND: University of North Dakota, 1986. Center for Innovation and Business Development, Box 8103, University Station, Grand Forks, ND 58202. (701) 777-3132. Instruction handbook.

Feasibility Checklist for Starting Your Own Business. SBA no. MA 2.026.

Guerrilla Marketing. Levinson. Boston: Houghton-Mifflin.

The Information Catalog. 500 Fifth Avenue, New York, NY 10110. Catalog.

Opening Your Doors: A Guide to Opening and Operating a Bed and Breakfast. Steven D. Brown. Small Business Development Center, University of Vermont Extension Service, Booklet 250.

Self-Employment Tax. Pamphlet no. 533. U.S. Department of the Treasury, Internal Revenue Service, Central Area Distribution Center, 2402 E. Empire, Bloomington, IL 61704.

Starting and Managing a Business from Your Home. Lynn Waymon. U.S. Small Business Administration, Starting and Managing Series, vol. 2, Washington, D.C., 1986.

Tax Guide for Small Business. Pamphlet no. 334. U.S. Department of the Treasury, Internal Revenue Service, Central Area Distribution Center, 2402 E. Empire, Bloomington, IL 61704.

Telecommunications
On-Line

CompuServe. A division of H&R Block. (800) 848-8199.

GEnie. A division of General Electric. (800) 638-9636.

The Source. A division of *Readers' Digest.* (800) 336-3366.

Expert

Peter Wheelwright, 125 Cedar Street, New York, NY 10006, (212) 619-2010.

VGM CAREER BOOKS

OPPORTUNITIES IN
*Available in both paperback and
 hardbound editions*
Accounting
Acting
Advertising
Aerospace
Agriculture
Airline
Animal and Pet Care
Architecture
Automotive Service
Banking
Beauty Culture
Biological Sciences
Biotechnology
Book Publishing
Broadcasting
Building Construction Trades
Business Communication
Business Management
Cable Television
Carpentry
Chemical Engineering
Chemistry
Child Care
Chiropractic Health Care
Civil Engineering
Cleaning Service
Commercial Art and Graphic Design
Computer Aided Design and
  Computer Aided Mfg.
Computer Maintenance
Computer Science
Counseling & Development
Crafts
Culinary
Customer Service
Dance
Data Processing
Dental Care
Direct Marketing
Drafting
Electrical Trades
Electronic and Electrical Engineering
Electronics
Energy
Engineering
Engineering Technology
Environmental
Eye Care
Fashion
Fast Food
Federal Government
Film
Financial
Fire Protection Services
Fitness
Food Services
Foreign Language
Forestry
Gerontology
Government Service
Graphic Communications
Health and Medical
High Tech
Home Economics
Hospital Administration
Hotel & Motel Management
Human Resources Management
  Careers
Information Systems
Insurance
Interior Design
International Business
Journalism
Laser Technology
Law

Law Enforcement and Criminal Justice
Library and Information Science
Machine Trades
Magazine Publishing
Management
Marine & Maritime
Marketing
Materials Science
Mechanical Engineering
Medical Technology
Metalworking
Microelectronics
Military
Modeling
Music
Newspaper Publishing
Nursing
Nutrition
Occupational Therapy
Office Occupations
Opticianry
Optometry
Packaging Science
Paralegal Careers
Paramedical Careers
Part-time & Summer Jobs
Performing Arts
Petroleum
Pharmacy
Photography
Physical Therapy
Physician
Plastics
Plumbing & Pipe Fitting
Podiatric Medicine
Postal Service
Printing
Property Management
Psychiatry
Psychology
Public Health
Public Relations
Purchasing
Real Estate
Recreation and Leisure
Refrigeration and Air Conditioning
Religious Service
Restaurant
Retailing
Robotics
Sales
Sales & Marketing
Secretarial
Securities
Social Science
Social Work
Speech-Language Pathology
Sports & Athletics
Sports Medicine
State and Local Government
Teaching
Technical Communications
Telecommunications
Television and Video
Theatrical Design & Production
Transportation
Travel
Trucking
Veterinary Medicine
Visual Arts
Vocational and Technical
Warehousing
Waste Management
Welding
Word Processing
Writing
Your Own Service Business

CAREERS IN Accounting; Advertising;
Business; Communications; Computers;
Education; Engineering; Health Care;
High Tech; Law; Marketing; Medicine;
Science

CAREER DIRECTORIES
Careers Encyclopedia
Dictionary of Occupational Titles
Occupational Outlook Handbook

CAREER PLANNING
Admissions Guide to Selective
  Business Schools
Career Planning and Development for
  College Students and Recent
  Graduates
Careers Checklists
Careers for Animal Lovers
Careers for Bookworms
Careers for Culture Lovers
Careers for Foreign Language
  Aficionados
Careers for Good Samaritans
Careers for Gourmets
Careers for Nature Lovers
Careers for Numbers Crunchers
Careers for Sports Nuts
Careers for Travel Buffs
Guide to Basic Resume Writing
Handbook of Business and
  Management Careers
Handbook of Health Care Careers
Handbook of Scientific and
  Technical Careers
How to Change Your Career
How to Choose the Right Career
How to Get and Keep
  Your First Job
How to Get into the Right Law School
How to Get People to Do Things
  Your Way
How to Have a Winning Job Interview
How to Land a Better Job
How to Make the Right Career Moves
How to Market Your College Degree
How to Prepare a *Curriculum Vitae*
How to Prepare for College
How to Run Your Own Home Business
How to Succeed in Collge
How to Succeed in High School
How to Write a Winning Resume
Joyce Lain Kennedy's Career Book
Planning Your Career of Tomorrow
Planning Your College Education
Planning Your Military Career
Planning Your Young Child's
  Education
Resumes for Advertising Careers
Resumes for College Students & Recent
  Graduates
Resumes for Communications Careers
Resumes for Education Careers
Resumes for High School Graduates
Resumes for High Tech Careers
Resumes for Sales and Marketing Careers
Successful Interviewing for College
  Seniors

SURVIVAL GUIDES
Dropping Out or Hanging In
High School Survival Guide
College Survival Guide

VGM Career Horizons
a division of *NTC Publishing Group*
4255 West Touhy Avenue
Lincolnwood, Illinois 60646-1975